THE HERITAGE OF

Huddersfield

THE HERITAGE OF
Huddersfield

Isobel Schofield

The Breedon Books
Publishing Company
Derby

First published in Great Britain by
The Breedon Books Publishing Company Limited
Breedon House, 44 Friar Gate, Derby, DE1 1DA.
1996

ISBN 1 85983 049 8

Printed and bound by Butler & Tanner Ltd., Selwood Printing
Works, Caxton Road, Frome, Somerset.

Colour separations by Colour Services, Wigston, Leicester.

Jackets printed by Lawrence-Allen, Weston-Super-Mare, Avon.

Contents

Acknowledgements

I would like to express my thanks to the staff at Huddersfield Local History Library and Tolson Memorial Museum for their help and patience as I have been involved in my researches. To the staff at the *Huddersfield Daily Examiner* office in Market Street, to Liz Hayes at the Central Graphics Unit and George Jackson for the many photographs that they have provided or printed up for this book.

A special word of thanks must go to those who have deposited their family photographs that have given us such a picture of the Huddersfield area at the end of the 19th century and most of all to the staff photographers at the *Huddersfield Examiner*. These dedicated men go out and about week by week in all kinds of weather to illustrate the many stories that appear in our daily paper. Their work at times must seem routine, but the result is a wonderful resource that brings to life the history of the town in all its aspects. They include in the latest generations: Andy Catchpool, Peter Cottle, David Hollingworth, Anthony Hodge, Julian Hughes, Bob Staniforth, John Watson and Paul Welch.

My thanks also go to Robert Drummond of the *Examiner* for his professional help in checking the text. Most of all they go to my husband for his help and encouragement as I spent the many hours needed to choose the photographs, research and write this book.

The Kirklees Photographic Archive

Kirklees Cultural Services, Museums and Arts section hold, with a deposit agreement, the *Huddersfield Daily Examiner* collection of negatives. These date from 1946 to the early 1980s and contain many of the photographs which appeared in the *Examiner* during these years.

In addition, the archive also contains a number of earlier collections acquired originally by individual museums now in Kirklees. These date from 1865 onwards and represent the work of both amateur and professional photographers. Within these collections images exist for every area of Huddersfield and many parts of Britain and Europe.

With the exciting new developments announced alongside, the Photographic Archive will be breaking new ground. Unfortunately for some time beforehand it is unlikely that the Archive will be accessible to the public, however arrangements have been made so that copies of the photographs used in this book from the Archive may be purchased (to order) through your local Kirklees library or museum.

Public Access to the Kirklees Photographic Archive

With a grant of £126,750 from the Heritage Lottery Fund, public access to the photographic collections will be revolutionised over the next few years. During 1998 user-friendly, touch screen computer terminals will be launched at a number of local museums and libraries to provide easy access to the fascinating photographic collections managed by Kirklees Cultural Services.

Michael Hall
Senior Registrar (Museums and Arts)

Introduction

Photographs of the 1890s to the 1990s bring to life some aspects of *The Heritage of Huddersfield*. We have a long and proud heritage in this area of West Yorkshire which deserves to be recorded.

The earliest settlers, the Romans, Anglo-Saxon and Norman invaders have all left their mark on the landscape and in the dialect words and village names that we use today. More modern settlers have changed the culture of the town. Polish and Ukrainian refugees after World War Two, and more recently the West Indian and Indian settlers looking for work, have all brought something of their own culture and added it to the native Yorkshire traditions.

I have tried to bring to life some of the changes, not only in the way of life, transport, education and health. But also some of the history of the many villages that surround the town and of the activities and traditions that enliven our daily routines.

Huddersfield changed greatly in the 1970s, not least in that Kirklees came into being, and I have shown something of those years, in comparison to the 1950s represented in *Images of Huddersfield*.

The photographs have all been taken from the Archive held by Kirklees Cultural Services, which includes collections from the end of the 19th century and the *Examiner* Archive which we hold up to the 1980s. More modern photographs are, on the whole, from the *Huddersfield Daily Examiner's* current collections.

It is inevitable that any book of photographs will reflect the interests of the author, constrained by what is actually available and the space within the book. I have quite deliberately tried to use photographs that have not been published in other books. Where subjects such as the Huddersfield Town AFC and Rugby Union have been covered in other books recently I have contented myself with an honourable mention.

There are so many photographs and subjects that could have been used, so please do not think I have deliberately missed your village or special interest – there just was not time, in some cases the photographs, or room in the book to cover everything.

As in *The Images of Huddersfield*, the story starts in the town centre, moves out to the areas of the county borough, then to the surrounding villages, before covering topics such as agriculture, industry, medicine, education and the cultural and community changes that have affected our lives.

Isobel Schofield

Huddersfield Town Centre – Past and Present

Storm clouds loom over Huddersfield town centre as the traffic races down Bradford Road towards Fartown Bar.
(Ex72.7802)

Huddersfield Market Place with its Market Cross is the central point of the town. The Cross dates from 1671 when Sir John Ramsden was awarded the Market Charter. As landowners of most of the town, the Ramsden family provided public wells to improve the water supply. On 12 June 1888 Sir William Ramsden donated a fountain to celebrate the Jubilee of Queen Victoria's reign. The Mayor is seen accepting this gift on behalf of the people of Huddersfield before the water was turned on by Lady Guendolen Ramsden. The fountain was later replaced by public toilets and moved to its current site in Greenhead Park. *(RH2/7)*

Market Walk is a passageway joining the Market Place with King Street. Colloquially known as 'Wappy Nick' there are still some of the later Victorian shop fronts to be seen such as on the jewellers, Geoff Neavy. Barker's supplied travel goods and sports clothing and equipment for many years on this site, moving to the corner of Queen Street and King Street before closing in March 1996.
(HX/33)

New Street in the early 1910s, the building on the right was replaced by what is now Lloyds Bank. The Halifax Joint Stock Bank merged with the Halifax and Huddersfield Union Bank in 1911 to form the West Yorkshire Bank who erected this building in 1912.   (KMC)

Erected between 1778 and 1790, Brick Buildings originally had little 'flat bow windows' but by 1846 only two or three remained. The buildings were refaced in the mid-19th century by bricks that had been bought, but were not required, for the erection of the Cloth Hall.   (RH2/10)

New Street looking towards the Market Place in the 1920s. Note the ornate Midland Bank on the left-hand side.
(M/0304)

The shop fronts have changed, but from a similar spot, the old New Street can still be seen today. The Midland Bank was rebuilt in the 1970s and the area was pedestrianised in 1993-94.   (c94 07 11-23)

Taken from Ramsden House, the picture shows the newly pedestrianised New Street with its complicated pattern of bricks which has proved popular with shoppers. To the right is the Prudential Building, which was constructed in terracotta brick rather than the more usual stone. It cost £9,260 in 1901 and was one of the last to be designed by Alfred Waterhouse as he retired soon after due to ill health. The ground floor, originally used as offices by Prudential, was converted to shops in 1938.   (Ex95-cv60)

Imperial Arcade was built in 1878 by J.R.Hopkinson, on the site of Hanson's yard. Named after the Imperial Hotel which stood on the opposite side of New Street, it was renovated during the the 1980s. It is still a popular thoroughfare from New Street to High Street and the bus station.   (Ex64/OH78 0054/1879)

Imperial Arcade following the renovations that has made it into such an attractive shopping area.   (KMC, 1990)

Buxton Road and the busy Huddersfield Industrial Society Co-operative store. Designed in 1893 by J.Berry in a mixed Renaissance style, it was officially opened in 1906. The 1936 extension by W.A.Johnson and J.W.Cropper is regarded as the best early example of modern architecture in the town. The Co-operative movement began in Meltham and extended to the town when the Huddersfield Co-operative Trading Association was formed in April 1829. Although the idea survived, many early co-operatives failed. In the second wave, the Huddersfield Industrial Society was founded in 1860 and went on to build the fine store in use today. (0054/1226)

Chapel Hill looking towards the Huddersfield Co-operative Society on Buxton Road in around 1900. The hill takes its name from the first Wesleyan Methodist Chapel built in Huddersfield which was closed in 1950. Next to the Chapel was the Model Lodging House, a converted warehouse in which nightly accommodation was supplied to the poor members of the community. Unusually it was supported by the rates, the lodging house was extended in 1897 to accommodate 186 beds and was in use until 1957. Photographed by Lewis Cousen (LC/28)

For many years, Ramsden Street was the centre of the town's municipal and cultural activities, being the home of the Theatre Royal, The Ramsden Street Baths, Ramsden Street Congregational Chapel, the Philosophical Hall, and many Council Departments. Princess Anne arrived at the Town Hall in 1973 when she came to open the new Sports Centre. In the background is Whitfield's furnishing store. In 1975 Barclay's Bank applied for permission to share the building with the store but the council turned the idea down at the time saying that the area was allocated primarily to shopping purposes and that the bank would be detrimental to the street.   (Ex73.4834)

The crowds gathered outside Huddersfield Town Hall on 10 May 1910 to hear the Mayor announce the Proclamation of the Accession of King George V.
                                                                                              (KCS)

The Town Hall has been used for many events over the years. The main hall was hired by the congregation of St Paul's Church in February 1889 who erected these elaborate decorations for a fund raising bazaar.   (RH5/32)

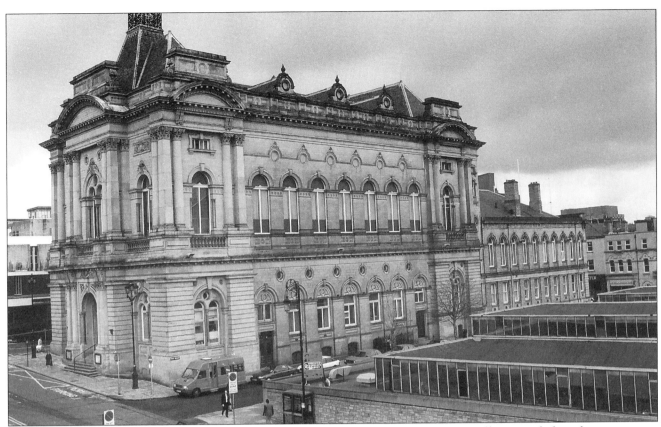

Huddersfield Town Hall, built in 1875-76 and extended in 1878-81, was originally intended to be temporary corporation offices. The concert hall dominates the building and has seen many important events and concerts, which include the annual Choral Society 'Messiah' performances.   (Ex95 cv)

The Hippodrome, designed by William Wallen, was originally built as a Riding School and Armoury in 1849 for the 2nd West Yorkshire Yeomanry Cavalry. It became the headquarters of the 2nd Volunteer Battalion of the Duke of Wellington's (West Yorkshire) Regiment until the Drill Hall on St Paul's Street was opened in 1901. The building was transformed by Miss Vesta Tilly into a Variety theatre, which opened in 1905, and became the Tudor House Super Cinema in 1930. After many name changes and a fire that destroyed part of the building, it is the Tudor Cinema once again. The Zetland Hotel originally opened as the Druid Hotel in 1849 and became O'Neill's Irish bar in 1995-96.   (SC/0108)

The old Philosophical Hall was destroyed by fire on 15 February 1880. Erected in 1833-34 the Hall was converted to the Theatre Royal which was demolished in 1961 to make way for the Piazza development. (RH2-32)

Ramsden Street Congregational Chapel was on the corner of Ramsden Street and Bull and Mouth Street. A daughter chapel of Highfield Congregational Church, it was designed by J.P.Pritchett at a cost of £6,500. In an attempt to boost congregations in the early years of the 20th century they held very popular lantern slide shows after the evening service. The first chapel in the town to be lit by gas, it was pulled down in 1934 and the Huddersfield Library built on the site. The income from the sale of the land was used to build a new Congregational Church on the Council Estate at Brackenhall. (RH3/48B)

Huddersfield Library and Art Gallery opened during World War Two in 1940. Early photographs show it surrounded by sandbags. Exciting suggestions were made in 1995 to extend the building to make use of space on the three sides and the central well which gives extra natural light to the reference, local studies and lending libraries.   (Ex95cv)

During summer, the Piazza provides a breath of fresh greenery in the centre of town and the steps are very popular with local people, eating their lunch or just enjoying 'people watching'. Work to revamp the area started in January 1996. The new Market Hall is the low building in the centre of the photograph.   (c94-06-23-13)

Queensgate Market was opened on 2 April 1970 to some complaints and nostalgia for the old hall. However, that did not stop the customers arriving. The *Examiner* headline read 'Chaotic! that's the verdict on the first day in Market'.
(Ex70.1753)

Car reversing lights and camping Gaz burners were just some of the methods used by enterprising stall holders when fuel shortages in 1973 resulted in power cuts. Mrs D.Hollingworth is seen serving Mrs D.Tedder with a pair of shoes by candlelight and a lighted butchers is in the background.
(Ex73.11585)

The Albert Hotel on Victoria Lane was designed by Edward Hughes. There is some interesting Victorian etched glass inside. For many years the *Examiner's* 'local', the Albert has been well patronised by town hall and library staff and has become well known within the 'Poetry Capital of the North' for its regular poetry readings and literary meetings.

(RH1/24)

Victoria Street is one of the many streets that vanished during the 1960s and '70s redevelopment of the town. Leading from Queen Street to Victoria Lane, the street included the back entrance to Market Hall and the Unicorn Inn. Beaumont's Warehouse, a trade warehouse which was once the Imperial Hotel also vanished at that time. Frank Fairburn & Sons Ltd on Victoria Lane was a leather goods shop.

(Ex.OH142.69)

Frank Fairburn in 1910 supplied cobblers with leather for shoe repairs, later expanding to travel equipment and fancy leather goods. In 1926 the firm supplied their strangest commission to a visiting circus when they were requested to make leather boots for an elephant. The firm closed down in August 1974 when the partners retired and the area redeveloped. From the left Mr J.Fairburn, Mr F.Fairburn and Mr C.Fairburn. (Ex74.5469)

The Shambles takes its name from the area of the town where animals were slaughtered for meat. Since this photograph was taken this area was redeveloped when the (old) Market Hall was built in 1880, although the name was kept for the road on the lower side of the building. The area was redeveloped again in the 1970s but its name is remembered in the walkway between W H Smith and Boot's. (RH3/22)

King Street in 1889 shows the Market Hall built in the Gothic style on the site of the old Shambles. Felt to be 'out of date' and too expensive to upgrade, it was demolished in 1970 and the site is now occupied by Boots and other retailers.   (RH5/10)

The demolition of the old Market Hall was struck by tragedy on 16 May 1970. The workmen were taking the tower down bit by bit when it suddenly collapsed. Mr Tom O'Toole of Almondbury and Mr Alan Watson of Dalton lost their lives, but Mr Raymond Walls jumped 15ft to safety as he felt the tower moving and shaking.   (Ex70.2876)

In 1964 this part of King Street was awaiting redevelopment. The firm of Thomas Kaye & Sons was originally Kaye and Monnington. The arched entrance led to the Pack Horse Yard and was pulled down in the 1970s. Kaye's Drapers sold every type of button and good quality and fashion clothing. Many readers will remember the way the money and receipts were sent overhead in a pneumatic tube in their shop on the top side of Market Walk. Kaye's closed in the 1980s but the management reopened as Peters of Huddersfield who have continued to provide an upmarket fashion service to the town.   (HLSA)

'Crispin's Corner' in 1889 was on the corner of King Street and Queen Street. The area was formerly covered by Dyson's Warehouse which was destroyed by fire. Queen Street contains a fine row of ashlar-faced Georgian houses. The Queen Street Mission standing back in Queen's Square is now the Lawrence Batley Theatre, next door, along the street, is the former County Court which is now a public house.   (RH5/11)

The east side of Cross Church Street in 1890 was a busy area with several public houses, some of which have survived to the present day.   (GH2/6A)

St Peter's Parish Church was erected in 1835-36 replacing a 1506 church built on the site. The architect, W.Exley of York, made use of the stone from the old building, unfortunately because the stone was placed the wrong way round, there have been maintenance problems ever since as it is easily eroded by the weather.   (SHB/8)

The Parish Churchyard was redesigned in 1951-52 to create St Peter's Gardens. Between 1584 and 1850 over 38,000 bodies had been buried in the graveyard of the Parish Church. So many that old graves were disturbed as new ones were dug, creating a stench and health risk. Therefore the new cemetery at Edgerton was opened in 1850. For many years, the local weavers had laid their 'pieces' of cloth for sale over the walls of the churchyard but the attendant stench and openness to the vagary of weather led to the development of many of the yards in the town and the Cloth Hall. (Ex1995 cv78)

Part of the Huddersfield Hotel complex includes the Boy and Barrel public house. According to one tradition, this pub was one of the few buildings in Huddersfield not owned by the Ramsden family. The head of the family, wanting to buy it, offered the landlord to cover the floor with sovereigns, 'Aye,' said the landlord 'if th'a stands them on th'edge'. Naturally this offer was not taken up! The boy sitting on his barrel was sent to the National Railway Museum in York to be restored and was re-erected in March 1996. (Ex2164-12a-96)

Rosemary Lane was a very old street of the town and is now remembered only by the name of the Rosemary Lane Bistro. The Huddersfield Hotel is well known in the town for its seasonal lights throughout the year and attractive floral displays in the summer.

(Ex cv 49)

The Palace Theatre was but one of several theatres in the town. Known for its Music Hall and lighter entertainment it is now used as a Bingo Hall.

(SC/1844)

One of the oldest roads in the town, Kirkgate, was the home of the Parish Church, a variety of inns and in the 1880s, fine new buildings that housed the Waverley Hotel and the Huddersfield Club. This photograph shows the 300-year-old Pack Horse Hotel and the entrance to the White Swan Yard in the early 1900s. (0054/1814)

The Pack Horse Centre was opened in the 1970s as part of Huddersfield's redevelopment. Refurbished in the 1990s, the centre has always been popular and provides a very useful shortcut from the Market Hall to the outdoor market now held on Byram Street. (c95 09 19-13a)

Busy Byram Street in the rain in 1972. The Kirkgate Buildings have now been restored and are used by Kirklees Council as office accommodation. (Ex72.7975)

Swan Yard was the scene of many political meetings including those of one of the earliest political associations in the town. Joshua Hobson and Richard Oastler were among those who attended the first meetings of the Huddersfield Radical Union. The first edition of *The Voice of the West Riding* was printed and published by Joshua Hobson in 1833 in Swan Yard. Swan Yard was demolished in 1879 to allow the development of Byram Street. At the time it was intended that this area should be the site of either the railway station of the Town Hall, but Kirkgate Buildings and Bulstrode Buildings were erected instead. (RH5/34)

Rushworth's bazaar was founded in 1875 by Mr Aquilla Rushworth. These buildings also housed the telephone exchange until just after World War One.   (KMC)

Miss Shirley Gibson is seen serving at the glove counter during the 'Men Only' shopping night at Rushworth's, giving husbands and boyfriends a chance to complete their Christmas shopping in 1957.   (Ex75.5208)

Byram Arcade in Westgate was built in 1880-81 as an extension to Byram Buildings for John William Ramsden. Much of its original wrought-iron work still exists. Run down by the 1970s, renovations in the 1980s cost £250,000 to create a thriving shopping centre again. Now an important part of the 'Poetry Capital of the North' it houses the Poetry Business and is central to other literary plans for the future.   (GH1/13)

A short but interesting alleyway, Byram Court between John William Street and Railway Street, was one of the many interesting parts in the central area of Huddersfield chosen by Dr David Kirby and Mr Ian Gouch, senior lecturers at the Polytechnic's Geography and Geology Department, to be included in their *Huddersfield Town Trail* published in 1974.
(Ex74.6330)

The interior of Byram Arcade in July 1994 shows the fine metalwork and restoration that make it such an attractive place to visit whether to shop, or to sit in and enjoy a coffee.   (c94 07 11-24a)

Westgate was once known as Top o'th Town. It has been redeveloped and prosperous over the years. This photograph was taken just before a road alteration scheme in 1932. The Swan with Two Necks Hotel was rebuilt and renamed the Royal Swan but the Wellington Hotel has changed little from the outside. Field's Café is remembered as a popular meeting place.

(HX/36)

Sergeantson Street from Westgate in the 1920s highlights the soot blackening effects of the industrial and domestic use of coal on the buildings. To the right the buildings have been cleaned and still house Wheawill and Sudworth Chartered Accountants upstairs, although the bank is now an Indian restaurant. The other buildings (including in the centre the Cloth Hall and to the left the Plough Inn, where the Huddersfield Choral Society is reputed to have been formed) have all been demolished.

(HX/72)

Cherry Tree Corner did not get its name from these flowering cherry trees but from the inn which stood on the site in the 1870s. Designed by W.H.Crosland it was favoured by clothiers visiting the town on market day.   (HLSA)

The buildings to the right of Westgate have changed little since this photo was taken in the 1920s. The trams have been replaced by the wide range of buses that make use of the new bus station. The buildings at the junction of Trinity Street and New North Road at the top of the picture have been demolished and replaced by the Ring Road, St Patrick's Centre and New North Road Baptist Church.   (KCS)

The St Patrick's Centre with the New North Road Baptist Church tucked in behind and the Technical College on the other side of the ring road. Photographed in 1995, they replaced the parade of shops shown in the centre of the previous photograph. (GRS 2181)

Peel Park was commonly known as Sparrow Park between Upperhead Row and George Street. As a result of a dispute, it was decided Peel statue would be erected in this park but the dispute was solved and it eventually was positioned in front of the station. The fountain at the centre of the park was originally intended to be in the Market Place, but was not considered to be important enough. To the right, George Street Chapel was built in 1855-56 at a cost of £2,500 for the Evangelical Union congregation and in the centre, Messrs Conacher's organ factory was built in 1859. This area is now part of the bus station. (RH5/64)

Railway Street was built in the 1870s and includes such fine architecture as Tite Buildings and the former Ramsden Estate Office which is still occupied by a variety of Council departments.   (GH2/29B)

Britannia Buildings in St George's Square were built as warehouses and offices in 1856-59. For many years the home of the Huddersfield Building Society it is now owned by the Yorkshire Building Society.   (M/350)

The George Hotel was built in 1849-50 to replace the George Inn which had been demolished making way for John William Street and St George's Square. The historic meeting that resulted in the foundation of the Rugby League took place in the hotel in 1895. For many years the Huddersfield Sunday School Union brought together children from all the churches and chapels in the town to parade and enjoy themselves with a tea and games. Taken in the early 1900s the children in this photograph are from Paddock Congregational Church and are followed by the Mount Pleasant Wesleyan Sunday School. Photograph by Lewis Cousen. (LC/18)

Huddersfield Station was designed by J.P.Pritchett and built by Joseph Kaye. The foundation stone was laid on 9 October 1846, a public holiday in the town. Completed in 1850, the building cost £2,000 but more recent restoration has cost much more. The façade was much admired by John Betjeman. In 1995 the scaffolding came down to show the newly cleaned and restored façade. (Ex cv 61)

St George's Square with the Lion Buildings on John William Street in the background. The steam tram to the right is of a type used in Huddersfield between 1883 and 1902. The steam engine had skirts on to prevent anyone falling under the wheels but the passengers travelled on the trailer. The Lion Buildings were erected by Samuel Oldfield in 1852-54 as an arcade of shops and warehouses. The lion on top was carved by John Seeley, but has since been replaced by a fibre-glass replica. John William Street provides a direct route from the Station to the Market Place and commemorates just one member of the Ramsden family that for so many years owned most of Huddersfield and played such an important role in the town's development. (Ex)

The Huddersfield Town Council erected a fountain in St George's Square to commemorate the County Borough of Huddersfield prior to the local government reforms of April 1974. Described as a 'monstrous fountain' by two lecturers at the Polytechnic School of Architecture, the fountain was removed in 1976 having fallen victim to traffic pollution. (Ex74.2112)

The Media Centre on Northumberland Street opened in 1995. These buildings were formerly occupied by Crowther's builders merchants and had been empty for several years. Now occupied by a wide range of media orientated businesses and the 'Window on the World' Café and Cyber Bar where a drink of coffee can be enhanced by 'Surfing the Internet'. (c95 09 06-10)

The name 'Shore Head' dates from the 16th century when there was a sewer or open culvert in the area leading down to the river. It has always been an important road junction and has changed greatly over the years. All the buildings on this photograph have since been demolished. In 1996 Sainsbury's supermarket was on the left and the Huddersfield University occupied land to the right of the photograph. (SHA/6)

Around the Borough

From Shore Head the Wakefield Road crosses over the canal and the River Colne at Aspley. In 1972 Huddersfield Corporation planned to terminate the Ramsden Broad Canal at Aspley Basin as a result of a road widening scheme. The canal was filled in to save between £10-20,000, the cost of a new bridge and the warehouses were demolished. Increased leisure interest in the canal led to the Council reopening the bridge in the 1980s. (Ex72.2945)

The Ramsden Canal was built in 1811 to help transport woollen cloth to the markets of the world. The Huddersfield Narrow Canal and Aspley Basin were busy in the 1870s but by the 1950s trade had declined. The area has now been redeveloped as a recreational facility and the canals reopened to leisure barges. As part of the building of the Sainsbury's supermarket, the canal side from Wakefield Road to Turnbridge was made into an attractive canal side walk.

(Ex95 cv63)

The River Colne powered many mills including the first Almondbury manorial mill, the King's Mill, so named for the purchase of the land by William Ramsden from the King in the 16th century.   (SC/0167)

The Somerset Bridge over the River Colne was opened in 1874. The extra land required, along with £1,000, were donated by Sir John Ramsden and the bridge named after his father-in-law, the Duke of Somerset.   (SC/0170)

Wakefield Road at Aspley in the early years of the 20th century. The Somerset Arms along with this block of cottages and shops have survived the many changes and road widening schemes.   (SC/0106)

Wakefield Road at Green Cross Corner changed dramatically in the 1990s when the new part of Wakefield Road was built. Tram lines and cobbles have been replaced, but some of the houses to the right of the picture have survived.
(RH7/19D)

Taken at the turn of the century, this photograph shows the children of Christ Church, Moldgreen who attended one of the many Sunday schools in Huddersfield which provided a religious education and played an important part in the social life of all the family. (SC/0338)

Ravensknowle Hall was donated to the people of Huddersfield by Legh Tolson in memory of his two nephews who died in World War One. The house was built between 1859 and 1862 by John Beaumont. The winter gardens in the front of this photograph were demolished soon after World War Two and the site built over when the Transport Gallery was erected in 1974. (Tolson)

The Waterloo Mission served an area that owes its name to a bridge built in 1819, named after Wellington's famous battle. The original Mission Room to the left was replaced by this fine building in the early 1900s. Since then two churches have been united to form St Michael and St Helen's on Fleminghouse Lane, opened in the 1970s. (HLSA)

The valley of the Fenay Beck has been subject to flooding for many years and until recently these fields and trees were undisturbed. Taken in the early years of the 20th century, this view looks across the Fenay Valley to Cowmes with Lascelles Hall in the distance. The large building to the right is Providence Chapel. (SC/0032)

In September 1931 flood waters washed away the walls and part of the roadway, and rushed through the mills in the Fenay Valley between Penistone Road and Spa Bottom. In recent years flood alleviation schemes have led to houses being erected on these fields and to the left of this picture, a new Morrison's supermarket (opened in 1995).   (HLSA)

The Star Hotel at Fenay Bridge in the early 1900s. The pub has changed little on the outside and the mill has been replaced by housing but today, customers still enjoy a warm welcome and the lovely views over the Fenay Valley.
(SC/0025)

Cottages in the hamlet of Longley cluster around the gabled roof of Longley Old Hall. Parts of Longley Old Hall date from 1577 and the building was the last part of the Ramsden Estate in Huddersfield to be sold. The Ramsden family moved in the 1870s to the Longley New Hall which became Longley Hall School for Girls and in 1996 is now Longley School.   (SC/0035)

The grounds of Longley New Hall played host to the Yorkshire Agricultural Show in August 1888. Opened on 7 August, over 66,000 people attended the show which was the largest number on record to that date. These grounds are now a very popular nine-hole golf course.   (RH4/37)

A very popular village to the south-east of Huddersfield, Almondbury was originally more important than Huddersfield. Turning up past the church towards Castle Hill some of these buildings in Westgate are still to be seen, although the Methodist Church was rebuilt in the 1970s when the two Methodist churches in the village united.

(SC/0023)

All Hallows Parish Church in Almondbury was built in 1470-1520 on the site of a previous church dating from before 1231. Since then there have been many alterations and the church was restored in 1872. One of the unique and notable features is the beautiful carved roof, dating from 1522. This photograph shows the interior of the church looking west before the 1875 restorations. The organ is said to have come from the Free Trade Hall in Manchester.

(RH1/9)

Almondbury as seen from the tower of All Hallows Church in August 1970. Looking across Northgate with the bus terminus to the left and Watercroft leading down to the right. The disused Watercroft mill overlooks the Almondbury Liberal Club's bowling green.   (Ex70.4409)

Not 'Dr Who's Tardis' but a miniature Police Station that served its purpose in 1980 when PC Michael Hield used the telephone to contact base. Once painted 'post office red' the Police Box was later painted blue and it is the only survivor in West Yorkshire of what was considered the peak of efficiency in 1936. (Ex80.11119)

So many of the 'Common' areas of Huddersfield have been lost over the years. This small part of Almondbury Common was fenced off and a plaque erected to record that at the Rush Bearing Festival the last local bull baiting took place on this site in 1824. (Ex72.2446)

There have been many archaeological digs on Castle Hill to try and prove the veracity of the many legends associated with the hill. Dr William Varley, leader of many such digs climbs up from the bottom of the well in August 1970. (Ex70.4763)

In front of the Victoria Tower is the beacon on Castle Hill which was originally used in 1588 to warn of the invasion of the Spanish Armada. This new beacon was erected in 1988 to celebrate 400 years of freedom. The Victoria Tower was built in 1899 to commemorate Queen Victoria's Diamond Jubilee – according to tradition the shape of the tower should look like Queen Victoria's profile when viewed from a certain angle, unfortunate repairs after lightening strikes have since destroyed the illusion. (Ex 1995)

This view of Castle Hill from Beaumont Park in the early 1900s, shows Lockwood Viaduct, Taylor Hill and dominant on the skyline, Castle Hill. The hill has been occupied since the Bronze Age. Various defences have been built over the years, but there is no evidence of Roman Occupation. A Norman castle was built on the site by Ilbert de Laci in the 1140s but demolished in 1340.   (M/0094)

Sheltering beneath the shadow of Castle Hill, Hall Bower School is one of the few remaining undenominational Sunday Schools to be in existence. The Sunday school and day school were set up in 1814 in order to tame the 'wild rough youth of the neighbourhood'. (SC/0377)

The newly-painted Hall Bower Chapel reopened in September 1980 celebrating a century of services held in this building. The original building was erected in 1814 and replaced in 1879. (Ex80.08527)

Primrose Hill Methodist Church on the corner of Stile Common Road and Malvern Road, looking towards the
woods of Ashenhurst and Lowerhouses.   (SC/0013)

Jackroyd Lane in Newsome still retains some of the charm that it had at the turn of the century.   (SC/0384)

Cobbled streets without traffic where children can play safely in Newsome. (SC/0375)

Once an attractive village, Berry Brow is now a suburb of Huddersfield. Like most areas it had its own Co-op Industrial Society from which almost anything could be bought. This steep cobbled road is Waingate leading up to the railway station. The sculpture at Berry Brow Station was rescued and sent to the National Railway Museum in York when the station was closed. It is now on display in Tolson Museum. A new station opened in 1989. (SC/0045)

Dominated by Salem Methodist Chapel, the cottages of Berry Brow cling to the hillside. (SC/0050)

Armitage Bridge from Beaumont Park. The valley had been owned by the Brooke family since the 16th century and they commissioned R.D.Chantrell of Leeds to design St Paul's Church in 1848. Chantrell also designed Armitage Bridge House in 1828 for Mr John Brooke. The family occupied the house until 1938, when it was requisitioned for the war efforts and later offered to the Council.   (M/146)

Beaumont Park, opened on 13 September 1883 by the Duke and Duchess of Albany, was the gift of Henry Frederick Beaumont of Whitley Beaumont. According to a newspaper report of the time one Yorkshire man shook the hand of the Duke and coolly asked 'How's t'mother' (Queen Victoria).   (GH2/35A)

A line on the planners map threatened to swallow the homes of several elderly people who were unhappy about the threat of compulsory purchase orders on their homes. The road widening scheme was intended to alleviate traffic problems caused by the building of a new housing development on Netherton Moor. Another casualty of the scheme was the Netherton Cross which was to be resited nearby.   (Ex74.1377)

Blackmoorfoot Road, Crosland Moor after it had been reconstructed for the electric tram service which commenced in 1901.

(0054/880)

The bridge at Lockwood carries the main road from Huddersfield through to Honley, Holmfirth and the Woodhead Pass. The bridge was rebuilt in 1908-09, and strengthened in 1995. The junction of Bridge Street, Lockwood Road and Meltham Road has long been a traffic bottleneck for which a wide variety of traffic schemes have been tried.

(SC/0398)

The Red Lion Inn at Lockwood Bar was demolished in 1938. The original deeds show the building was erected in 1722 and it is known that John Horsfall was the innkeeper in 1741. The Red Lion over the years has been a focal point for Lockwood, the council met there until the Lockwood town hall was built in Swan Lane. The Bentley Charity was operated from the Inn, and the poor came there to collect their payment. The first local horse-drawn bus service operated from the pub.

(SC/0421)

Repairs and road works have always caused problems for travellers and pedestrians. In 1956 these pavement repairs in Bridge Street, Lockwood were being checked by mason brick layer Alf Usher. (Ex56.4638)

The busy junction of Longroyd Lane and Manchester Road at Longroyd Bridge in the 1960s. In the distance is St Thomas's Church which was built by local mill owner Sir Thomas Starkey and his brothers who died before it was completed in 1859. Across the junction was the tramway depot which had its own power station. (HLSA)

A lovely way to send a beautiful September day in 1956. Oddy's Ice Cream cart was photographed in the Paddock area for the *Examiner* feature 'Out and About with a Cameraman'.　　　　　　　(Ex56.4250)

The Paddock area was largely owned by the Ramsden Estate. All Saints Parish Church was built 1833, but was closed when the building became unsafe. The Anglicans now worship in the Shared Church which developed as the result of the coming together of the Methodist and the United Reformed Church. This photograph shows Paddock Vicarage in the late 1880s or 1890s.　　　　　　　(GH2/43C)

The bowling green at Paddock Cricket and Bowling Club was a favourite rendezvous point on a fine afternoon. This picture taken in August 1956 shows Mr Albert Stevenson and Mr J.McGrath watching Mr Harry Hirstwood and Mr John Hepson measuring the distances between the bowls and the jack. (Ex56.4244)

Milnsbridge takes its name from a bridge near the Longwood township's corn mill on the side of the River Colne. Renowned for its textile mills along the canal side such as Crowther's. Milnsbridge House, once set in a beautiful valley with fine gardens, is now run down and surrounded by industry. It was the home of Sir Joseph Ratcliffe JP scourge of the Luddites who investigated the murder of William Horsfall. Harold Wilson (Lord of Rievaulx and Kirklees) was born and raised in this area. (M/141)

Mills light up the night sky to show that these mills at least had plenty of work in the 1970s.   (HLSA)

The Roman Fort at Slack, near Outlane has been the scene of several archaeological excavations including those of 1865-66, 1913 and 1962. The site had defensive walls and ditches and included a selection of buildings including the Headquarters, regimental shrine, treasury and a well to supply water. The fort guarded the road between Manchester and York.   (Ex69.1749)

Nont Sarah's Hotel on the moors beyond Outlane was run by licensee Ernest Randall in 1974. He kept a log of the weather as a graph for trade purposes. The pub's unusual name comes from a corruption of the word Aunt. Legend has it that a local man who kept a pub in Lancashire wanted to buy the Coach and Horses, as it was known, and borrowed the money from his Aunt Sarah. It became known as Nont Sarah's and the name officially changed by Mrs Sykes, the next licensee who became 'fed up' with it being misnamed.   (Ex74.1405)

During the 1970s it was realised that much of our architectural heritage could be lost in the redevelopment of our towns and villages. Consequently many of the older parts of Huddersfield were listed and subject to special planning restrictions. Quarmby Fold is a fine example.   (HLSA)

There are many mills in the Oakes and Lindley areas including the Wellington Mills on Plover Road. These workmen are laying cobbles on Plover Road in around 1910 with Wellington Mills in the background. (M/144)

In *Words on War* by Helga Hughes there is a photograph showing a map of the Oakes and Lindley area of Huddersfield that was marked up for German bomber pilots. On the map is Wellington Mills which was damaged by a parachute mine on 23 December 1940. This photograph was donated to the Local History Library by Mr L.Scott.
(0054/2063)

Lidget Street, Lindley in the early 1900s. A village on the outskirts of Huddersfield, the name Lindley comes from 'Lin Leah' meaning a flax clearing. The Art Nouveau architect Edgar Wood designed several buildings in the area including the Clock Tower and Banney Royd. The Huddersfield Royal Infirmary moved to Acre Street in the 1970s. (SC/0268)

Trinity Street meets Westbourne Road at the Junction Roundabout. This photograph is taken from the hill called Snodley, where until recently there was a service reservoir. The Gledholt Methodist Church is on the right with the Ambulance Station next door. (Ex81.6519)

Greenhead Hall was owned by Benjamin Haigh Allen, the estate was sold to the Ramsden family following his death in 1829. Bought for the town, the grounds were redesigned by the Borough Surveyor, R.S.Dugdale and opened as Greenhead Park in 1884. Greenhead Hall was demolished in 1909 and the site used for Greenhead High School for Girls, now Greenhead College. The swans on the lake in Greenhead Park were donated by Sir John William Ramsden.

(RH6/14c)

Civic pride was reflected in the opening of the Richard Oastler Playground in Greenhead Park in the 1920s. Oastler had fought for the Ten Hours Bill and for children's rights as they worked in the factories. It is interesting to see the attitudes of the times – the playground was for children under nine years old and was closed on Sundays! (HLSA)

Dutch Elm disease stuck down many fine trees in Huddersfield, none more so than the avenue in Greenhead Park. Special protective measures were announced in 1975 but unfortunately all the trees were eventually attacked. Some stumps remain and have been carved and left as outdoor works of art. (Ex75.6364)

The Springwood area was laid out in the early 1800s as a wealthy residential suburb. Many parts of the area have been restored and adapted to today's needs with a sympathetic eye. Spring Street has changed little during the years since it was erected in the early 1800s. At the top of the street were the Waterworks offices built in front of the Spring Street Tank. This reservoir was built in 1743 by Sir John Ramsden, taking water from the nearby River Colne and a pumping station at Folly Hall. By the 1820s it was inadequate and new reservoirs were built in Longwood. (RH2/28)

Taken in 1968, this photograph reflects the immigration that has introduced so much diversity to the town. One of the most important inhabitants of Spring Street, Charles Sikes, lived at No.46 and was founder of the Post Office Savings Bank. In recent years restoration of the cobbled street and Victorian style lampposts have restored the street to its original appearance.   (HLSA)

The Ring Road cut the town centre off from other areas of Huddersfield, Springwood was no exception. New buildings and careful restoration has brought back to life what had become a very neglected, run down part of the town. This view from the bus station shows not only the new buildings dominated by Spring Grove School but the large car parks that are so essential in today's world. Elim Chapel to the right was extended in the late 1980s to accommodate a growing congregation.   (Ex cv 50)

Edgerton Cemetery was opened in 1855 to relieve the overcrowded Huddersfield Parish Church cemetery. Deliberately sited so that any smell would be carried away from the very desirable wealthy residential area of Edgerton occupied by the 'wool barons' and wealthy merchants of the town. (RH1/35)

Cottages at the Rocks, Birchencliffe in the early years of the 20th century. Birchencliffe is an area of the town on the main road to Halifax. By 1911 trams, and later trolley buses, passed through the area to connect Huddersfield with Elland and Halifax. (SC/0259)

The last electric tram on the West Vale route at Birchencliffe on 27 May 1939, passing through, what was described in 1972 as, a mini Khyber Pass when the *Examiner* reported that Halifax Road was in urgent need of widening.
(WBS/86)

Known as the `Teapot Chapel', Hillhouse Methodist Chapel was built in the 1870s. Its name either reflects the 'urn' prominently displayed on the top of the roof or the way that funds were raised by the chapel teas. Empty since 1962, according to the *Examiner* of 30 August 1972, the Anjuman Islamia, a Pakistani Community Association, wanted to buy the chapel to open an Islamic Centre.
(RH3/56D)

The *Examiner* feature 'Out and about with a Cameraman' visited this fish and chip shop in Birkby in 1956. The *Examiner* commented 'What a lovely place this shop is for husbands who have to cope with dinner when the wife is away'. They could buy tripe from Mrs Marian Crosley or fish and chips from Mrs G.Richardson on the right.

(Ex56.5259)

Children playing outside cottages at Netheroyd Hill. (SC/0321)

Fixby Hall was the home of the Saville family, but its greatest claim to fame was that Richard Oastler lived there as steward to the Thornhill estate between 1820-1838. He opposed the new Poor Law Amendment Act of 1834, was a candidate for Parliament, author of the Fleet Papers and other publications. He was involved in agitation to reform laws relating to factory conditions and child labour. The estate and hall are now owned by the Huddersfield Golf Club.   (SC/0334)

Woodhouse Hill climbs from Fartown Green to Sheepridge. An open agricultural area in around 1900. The Fartown High School now occupies much of the land to the right of the picture, behind buildings on Red Doles Road. Central Avenue is halfway up the hill.   (RH6/10B)

A delivery man with his horse prepares to deliver his goods in Sheepridge Road in the early 1900s. Note the meat hanging outside the butchers to the left of the photograph. (SC/0249)

A bad storm hit Huddersfield on 2 July 1968, causing much damage. These stalwarts of the Avenue allotments in Fartown are carrying out repairs on their greenhouse. From the left: Mr L.Livesey, Mr F.Kershaw and Mr B.Sunderland.
(HLSA)

Sheepridge Road Laundry photographed in the early 1900s. The building was still in use up to 1962. The laundry concern was taken over by another laundry firm in the same area. The building was taken by Mr Laurence Batley in 1958, at a rental of £260 for his expanding cash and carry business. When he opened his purpose-built buildings in 1962 these were demolished as part of a road widening scheme. (SC/0250)

Newhouse Hall, Deighton in 1903. Purchased by Sir John William Ramsden in 1854 the first tenant was Godfrey Binns of Deighton. At that time the house was in poor condition and the estate contributed towards the cost of the repairs to the extent of £130 for which 5 per cent was added on to the rent. (RH3/51)

olne Bridge takes its name from the river crossing built by the monks of Fountains Abbey. The river was also important
the Industrial revolution to provide power for the many mills. These mills are in the river valley along the River Colne
Colne Bridge.   (SC/0081)

Leeds Road at Colne Bridge in the early years of the 20th century.   (SC/0080)

The Wider Circle

Kirkheaton Carnival in 1905 when the villagers paraded through the streets. Kirkheaton is still known for its annual 'Yetton Rant' which takes place every Spring Bank Holiday in a field behind the Beaumont Arms. (120/435-2)

Cockhill's grocers shop in Kirkheaton in the early 1900s. The many village grocers shops not only seemed to sell all types of foods and groceries but they also delivered to the door. (120/435-9)

The George and Dragon in Flockton is an old timbered public house that has served the village for many years.

(0054/2085)

Plenty of rainclouds but the sun is shining to bring spring warmth to the centre of Flockton in March 1970. Among the trees is St James's Church.

(Ex70.1085)

A combination of fog and frost in March 1967 caused the 1,264 foot television mast at Emley Moor to collapse under the weight of ice, narrowly missing workmen who had just left the site. The noise of the collapse was heard for miles but the thick fog prevented the seriousness of the situation being realised until it cleared.   (Ex69.1215)

Damage to the Emley Moor Methodist Church is seen through the fog that had caused a build up of ice on the Emley Moor Mast. Two people inside the church had lucky escapes but the roof and organ were seriously damaged.
(Ex69.1213)

The new stronger mast which, at 1,084ft, is the tallest free standing concrete structure in Europe, was built much to the dismay of locals who had hoped that it would be built elsewhere. Norman Hirst of Lenacre Farm and 12-year-old Prince scuffle (clean) between rows of potatoes in the shadow of the new Emley Moor mast in June 1974. (Ex74.3868)

On Saturday, 31 September 1972, a group of walkers, from four-year-old Christopher Moorhouse to 74-year-old Willie Brooks, took part in the traditional Emley Boundary Walk. Some of the young people waded through the bed of the River Dearne near Park Mill where it forms part of Emley's boundaries. (Ex72.6814)

Brookhouse Dam, Clayton West with the Railway Junction in the background taken between 1900 and 1910. The village is on the outskirts of Kirklees between Holmfirth and Wakefield. It is no longer served by the railway as the line closed in 1983. But the Kirklees Light Railway is now redeveloping the line as a scenic route.　(TM/7AS)

The road winding through Skelmanthorpe in the early 1900s. According to a report in 1886 there were two lights at Kitchenroyd, one at the Co-op Butchers, one at Nortonthorpe and one at Geoffrey Lodge's yard at Buster. It was ordered that 'the lamps shall not be lit when the moon gives sufficient light for the safety of people and carriage traffic passing through the streets'.　(SC/102)

Skelmanthorpe, Grove Pub in the summer of 1980. (Ex80.08201)

The Penistone Line passes through Denby Dale, the railway cutting and viaduct were originally opened on 1 July 1850 but the viaduct was made of wood. Travellers were afraid and in 1880 a new stone viaduct was opened and carries the line 1,000 yards across the valley. (Ex54.3644)

These old men sitting in Denby Dale War Memorial Park put the world to rights as they sit and enjoy themselves in August 1954. From the left are Messrs H.Lockwood, B.Hanson, J.T.Dyson, F.Fitton and W.Haigh.　　(Ex54.3650)

The corner of Shelley Bank Bottom has been the scene of many accidents over the years. However, in the early 1900s it looked to be a very peaceful rural setting. The village of Shelley has extended in recent years and has become part of 'commuter land'. Shelley Hall and Gryce Hall are two of the old local houses that have been restored. It is a local tradition for residents to walk the boundaries every New Year's Day.　　(SC/0097)

Smoke rising from cottages in Thunder Bridge captured by Tom Mosley in the early 1900s.   (TM/3A)

The view across the village of Kirkburton towards All Hallows Church in 1972.   (Ex72.2439)

The Conservation area at Low Town, Kirkburton means that developers must pay more respect to the style of buildings erected which have to be in keeping with the old attractive cottages in George Street.   (Ex80.8474)

A new library at Kirkburton was opened on 14 July 1994. Previously staff and library users had struggled for many years in a converted terrace house, with steep steps leading to the door. Opened by the Mayor and Mayoress of Kirklees, there were many activities for children and visits from authors during the opening celebrations that were enjoyed by all. The new library has continued to grow in popularity. A specially designed stained glass window was installed in 1995 in the entrance to the building.   (c94 07 14-2/12)

The ancient village of Farnley Tyas was mentioned in the *Domesday Book* as *Fereleia*. The village was owned by the Dartmouth family until the entails were recently broken so that the land could be sold, instead of being passed down to the eldest son. Parts of Golden Cock are over 400 years old and it was this public house that was the focus for celebrations on 22 June 1897 when the village joined with the rest of the country to celebrate Queen Victoria's Diamond Jubilee. (120/405-9)

For many years Farnley Tyas has been a farming village. In 1972 the village residents decided to enter the best-kept village of West Yorkshire for the first time. The village was praised, but told that there was still some long standing litter problems to be solved. This more unusual view of the village is taken from the churchyard looking towards the Golden Cock which is just visible behind the trees. (Ex79.6365)

Tom Mosley of Shepley visited Woodsome Hall between 1900 and 1910 to give us this glimpse of the dining room. (TM/17a)

Woodsome Hall for many years was the home of the Dartmouth family. Built by the Nottons it passed to the Kaye family and later the Earls of Dartmouth. The Dartmouth's let the house to the Woodsome Hall Golf Club in the 1920s and subsequently sold it to them. Gardeners are seen cutting the grass outside Woodsome Hall in the 1890s with a horse-drawn mower. (M/126)

Woodsome Mill has stood on this site for over 800 years and was an important part of the Farnley Tyas manorial estate. Water was brought along a goit to the mill wheel. Taken in the early years of the 20th century the mill had not changed much when the *Examiner* reporter visited it in 1952. At that time it was owned by Mr Richard Redfern, whose family had run the mill since 1678. The mill had last been worked by his father but the milling equipment was removed in 1966 so that the building could be used as a barn. Later it was converted to a very attractive house.
(HLSA)

The machinery in the Woodsome Corn Mill stood ready to grind the wheat for local people in 1952 as it had for over eight centuries.
(Ex52.2217B)

Shepley was described as 'poor, proud and peevish' by its Shelley neighbours according to *Villages of South & West Yorkshire*. As recorded in *Images of Huddersfield*, the village contained many tailors who used the high quality local cloth to create suits. Tom Mosley took this photograph of the villagers of Shepley as they flocked out into the street to celebrate the Coronation of King George V in 1902.

(TM/17B)

Shepley Croquet Club was visited in October 1978 by *Examiner* reporter Susan Mellor. Feeling that if 'Alice could do it' she joined club members to learn how to play a game she describes as involving 'skill, judgment, accuracy and a certain amount of spite'. Mrs L.Hinchliffe was explaining the finer points of the game to Susan.   (Ex78.5328)

Snow causes havoc on the roads in the latter part of the 20th century. We may think that in earlier years they did not have the same problems, but this horse-drawn snowplough was used to clear the roads on 6 March 1909 in the village of Shepley. (TM/21B)

Frost enhances the view over the village of Thurstonland from the road that leads to Farnley Tyas. Clustered around St Thomas's Parish Church the village has a very popular pub, the Rose and Crown and an equally popular Cricket Club. (Ex76.4434)

Set in the valley at Jackson Bridge, Dobroyd Mills was very busy in the early years of the 20th century. By 1974 the *Examiner* was reporting that the contents of the mill 'were under the hammer' and expected to fetch about £150,000.
(HGB/001)

The name of Coal Pit Gate, New Mill reminds us of the heritage of these valleys where coal was used to power the mills. The first scribbling engine in the Holme Valley was installed at New Mill in 1780 and the surrounding hillsides are riddled with old coal and iron workings. (SC/0186)

New Mill from Greenhill Bank in the early years of the 20th century. (SC/0185)

A new lending library was opened in New Mill in 1975. Previously the library had been down a flight of steep dark steps. The prefabricated building cost £12,000 and was expected to last 20 years. Mrs J.Holmes (branch librarian) and Mr Gerry Peach (team leader) are examining one of the new books. (Ex75.8246)

Thongsbridge is one of the many small villages that owes its origin to the existence of a river crossing and the development of water to power the local mills. (SC/0216)

Brockholes, the 'land of the badgers' is dominated by outcropping rocks that give Rock Terrace its name. The corner shop, then a Co-operative, still sells provisions to local people. The Rock Mills were demolished in 1975. (SC/0222)

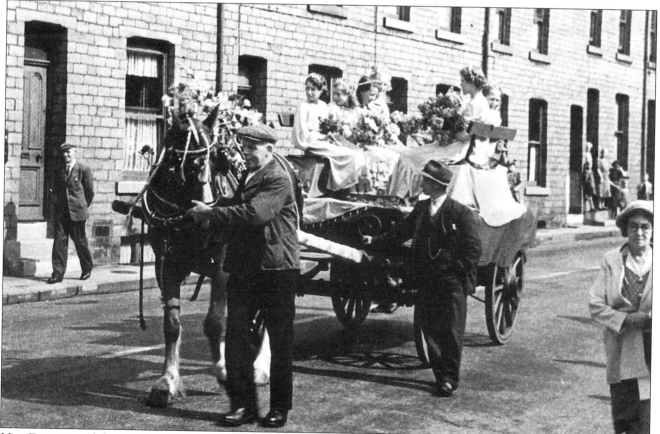

May Day was celebrated in style in c.1938 when this procession wound its way through Brockholes. George Senior, on the pavement, is watching Harold Gelder leading the horse and, among the girls on the float are Mary Nosley, Margaret and Joan Durrans, Kathleen Bullar and Laura Kinder.

(120/384-7)

The villagers of Butterley and Fulstone were hoping that large parts of the village would be designated as Conservation Areas when this photograph of an interesting corner in Butterley was taken in August 1980.

(Ex80.7833)

The main route into the centre of Honley climbs up the steep road known as Towngate. The horse troughs hint at the principle mode of transport during the early years of the century.

(120/303-5)

'It's Honley feast and the fair's in town!', said the *Examiner* in 1962 as these Honley children enjoyed the roundabout and holiday from school. As a custom the Feast may have been struggling in 1962, but it is popular in 1996 and many people still enjoy this September break. (Ex62.3943)

Holmfirth at the turn of the century, with its streets climbing the steep hillsides from the river valley. (SC/706)

The Upperbridge at Holmfirth as recorded in the *Huddersfield Chronicle* on 21 February 1852 showed the scene of desolation following the bursting of the Bilberry reservoir on 5 February 1852 when 81 people were drowned.
(0054/1799)

'Card sharp – he's got to be joking'. 62-year-old Arnold Taylor of Bamforth's in Holmfirth spent his days drawing all those wonderful comic postcards that we look at or buy at the seaside. He kept a diary of jokes that occurred to him or that people told him, then added the right illustration, scrapping about half of his ideas as he went along. Bamforth's was taken over by Dennis of Scarborough and production was moved there in 1995. The Postcard Museum, above Holmfirth Library, has displays of some of the many postcards in the collections and shows some of the original lantern slides and films from the time that Holmfirth was the 'Hollywood' of England.   (Ex73.8470)

In 1978 the Vicar of Holmfirth, Revd John Sausby, offered the church jail for sale. Known as the 'Tauser' in the church inventory in more recent years it had been used as a mortuary, fire station and latterly a garage. The vicar was offering the jail to the Civic Society, who believed that it could be the oldest building in Holmfirth, to ensure that it survived and was maintained. (Ex78.790)

One of the many busy markets around the Huddersfield area, Holmfirth's markets are held on Thursdays and Fridays with special craft markets on Bank holidays and Saturdays from March to Christmas.　(c93 06 17-41)

Nestling in the shadow of Holme Moss, Holme is the highest village in the Holme Valley. A 'Graveship', it was run by its own enterprising council who installed electricity in 1915 and had its own gas works until 1937.　(Ex53.2328)

A true Yorkshire village on the hillside above Holmfirth, Netherthong in 1954 was described as 'very much a community on its own'. But regular bus services meant that villages could reach both Huddersfield and Holmfirth easily. The centre of the village was described as being at the junction of three main roads to Meltham, to Deanhouse Hospital and to Holmfirth.   (Ex54.2650)

Upperthong dates from Saxon times and was ideal for textiles with sheep and good clean water. The Sunday School founded in 1837, became a day school for 40 children and is now the village hall. This attractive village seen in the early years of the 20th century is now a conservation area.   (KCS)

Marsden from Butterley Reservoir was a busy mill town when this photograph was taken at the turn of the century. Shown as 'March-dene' in old documents, the village was part of the lands given to Ilbert D'Laci in 1056. The village played an important role in the Industrial Revolution, with road, canal and rail transport passing through on their way over the Pennines.   (SC/791)

In 1973 Marsden's ancient stocks were repositioned in Town Gate where they were originally used in mediaeval times. Mr John George Sykes's last job as a stone mason for the Highways Department was to dismantle the stocks which had been moved to Marsden Park and rebuild them on the original site.   (Ex73.8629)

Some endearing features of many of the older parts of the towns and villages in the area are the ginnels and snickets that provide short cuts from one street to another. This ginnel in Meltham was photographed in March 1974.

(Ex74.1403)

Marsden celebrated its Rush Bearing festival in the rain in August 1980. The wide range of activities included a display in the Mechanics Hall, a procession with Morris Men, Majorettes and the village's own silver band. Ron Yates of Saddleworth Morris Men enjoyed his well earned refreshment having helped pull the Rush Cart around the village.

(Ex80.8383)

'Collop time is here again' was the heading in the *Examiner* in February 1978. Mrs Annie Woodhead, owner of a Meltham newsagent and tobacconist shop, gave away sweets and chocolate to village children on their way to school. The old tradition of giving food on Collop Monday, the day before Shrove Tuesday, started with farmers giving 'collops' of bacon to the villagers. Over the years this changed to local shopkeepers giving sweets to the children.   (Ex78.792)

The shopworkers await their customers outside Meltham Co-operative Society in the early years of the 20th century. The clock tower stands above Meltham Town Hall.   (SC/689)

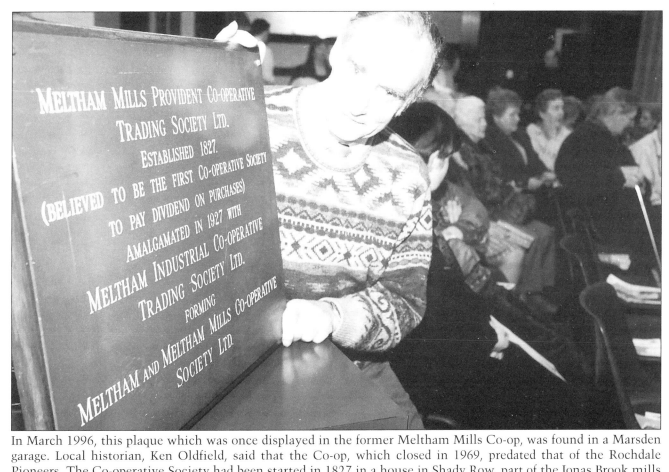

In March 1996, this plaque which was once displayed in the former Meltham Mills Co-op, was found in a Marsden garage. Local historian, Ken Oldfield, said that the Co-op, which closed in 1969, predated that of the Rochdale Pioneers. The Co-operative Society had been started in 1827 in a house in Shady Row, part of the Jonas Brook mills complex and moved to a shop in Meltham Mills Road two years later. One of the early members took the idea to Rochdale, having walked there to take up employment.   (Ex96.2511-36a)

Sheltered from the east and westerly winds, Helme was a popular weaving community but not industrialised. The name comes from the Saxon, meaning cattle shelter. The village's first entry in the best-kept village of West Yorkshire failed in 1979. It was praised as a very promising entry, with a special mention for the schoolchildren who had helped tidy the school garden and the churchyard.   (Ex79.6370)

Slaithwaite was once a very busy town that drew visitors from Lancashire and Yorkshire for 100 years from 1825. First records of Slaithwaite show that the Manor was owned by Kirklees Priory and that Henry Tyas paid a mark (two-thirds of a pound) for the use of the mill in c.1211. Britannia Road in Slaithwaite in 1953 still shows some the austerity of the war years.   (Ex53.2154)

This aerial view of Slaithwaite in 1984 clearly shows the development of the various forms of transport and how they affected the area. River, road, canal and railway have all played an important part in the shaping of the town. The needs of industry are reflected, water, first from the river then the mill dams and the rows of houses for the workers that creep up the hillside.   (Ex 8421/33A)

Terraced cottages line the cobbled street of Town End in the hillside village of Golcar in the early years of the 20th century.   (SC/711)

Crimble Clough is one of the most attractive parts of the Colne Valley and is near Slaithwaite. The Anglo-Saxon name means a small piece of land or water. (Ex74.4399)

Rural and Industrial Heritage

Nineteenth-century farming was labour-intensive and had not changed much since the times of the Enclosure Acts of the 17th century. The large 'common' fields were enclosed by walls in many cases by the local wealthy landowners. These cows are grazing the field near Fletcher House Farm, Almondbury in 1891. (M/0074)

The yearly round of ploughing, sewing the seed and harvesting the crops must have been very hard work, in the bitter cold of winter or in the heat of summer. This team of horses and the three men are seen mowing the hay at Woodsome in 1891. (M/0120)

Where the horse-drawn machinery was not considered suitable, teams of workmen would cut the hay with scythes. These workmen are sharpening their scythes with strickle boards. (M/0129)

The cut hay was left to dry and turned on several occasions before being collected and taken to be stacked at Fletcher House Farm, Almondbury. (M/0073)

The loaded haycart would then be taken to the farm or wherever the farmer chose to make his stack. These men are loading the haycart near Woodsome in 1891.   (M/0131)

The hay was stacked and thatched for use in the winter at Fletcher House Farm, Almondbury.   (M/0089)

Straying animals have always been a problem. Farmers solved this by the use of a 'pinfold' where any stray beast would be kept until claimed by its owner. This pinfold is at Wilberlee near Marsden and was photographed in 1964.

(HLSA)

More and more mechanisation was introduced in the 20th century. Potatoes that once were dug by hand, were turned over by tractors pulling a 'potato digger', although there was still the hard labour of picking them up. This potato digger was on a farm in the Scissett area.

(HLSA)

The harvest is now brought home ready baled to be stacked in the barn. This straw was being taken home to Tenter House Farm, Denby Dale in 1975. From the left are: Philip Geldart, David Gill and Andrew Mallinson, the tractor driver is Stephen Mallinson.   (Ex75.7805)

A tractor and baling machine meant in 1974 that Keith Morritt of Emley could do the same work that would have taken several men to do less than 50 years previously.

(Ex74.4802)

The many changes on the local farms are not only the result of mechanisation but of advances in how feed for the animals is stored. Silos such as this at Bentley Grange Farm at Emley have appeared on most farms in the area.   (Ex74.5879)

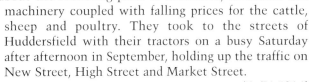

The mid-1990s have been hard for farmers with the health fears affecting sales of beef and other products. But farmers have always had problems and in 1974 protested about the rocketing price of foodstuffs, fertilisers and machinery coupled with falling prices for the cattle, sheep and poultry. They took to the streets of Huddersfield with their tractors on a busy Saturday after afternoon in September, holding up the traffic on New Street, High Street and Market Street.

(Ex74.5914)

Over the years it has been found that the natural teazel was best for raising the nap on cloth. In 1973 Edmund Taylor (Teazels) Ltd of Moldgreen was short of teazels and encouraged Huddersfield people to grow them.

(Ex73.10031)

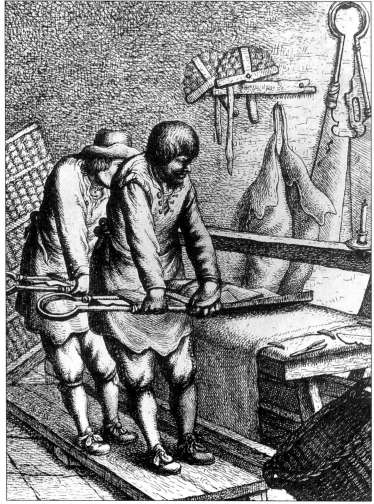

John Wood's Cropping Shop at Longroyd Bridge. The Huddersfield area was at the cutting edge of the use of new technology in the early years of the Industrial Revolution. Naturally these changes caused much hardship and unrest. The Luddites who attacked several mills in the area included a group of workers at John Wood's Cropping Shop. In April 1812 George Mellor, William Thorpe and Thomas Smith, plotted to kill William Horsfall, owner of Ottiwells Mill, Marsden. They were caught and hanged at York in January 1813.

(RH2/33C)

Croppers wielded 4ft long shears that weighed 40 pounds to finish the cloth by shearing off the raised nap. They were highly paid and resented the introduction of the new shearing frames that needed little skill or strength to operate.

(120/244-3)

The Dumb Steeple at Cooper Bridge on the boundary of Huddersfield, Mirfield and Brighouse may originally have been a 'Doom Steep', a mediaeval place of sanctuary. It is remembered as the place where the Luddites met before marching to attack the Rawfolds Mill in Liversedge. (RH6/22D)

Richard Oastler was the land steward at Fixby Hall who played a leading role in the Factory Movement following the publication of his letter on 'Yorkshire Slavery' in the *Leeds Mercury* in 1830. (KMC)

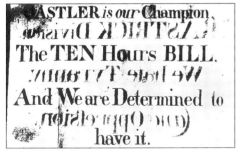

Work for the Ten Hours Bill led to the accusation that Richard Oastler was neglecting the Fixby Hall Estate. Supporters of Oastler marched in protest from Fixby Hall to Queen Street on 25 August 1838 carrying this flag, which is now in Tolson Museum. (KMC)

Following the massacre at Peterloo in Manchester, there was an upsurge of groups wanting Parliamentary Reform in this area and banners such as this one were carried to protest meetings. On display in the Tolson Museum the Skelmanthorpe Flag, a Chartist banner from the around 1819, was woven on a hand-loom by Mr Bird. He dedicated the flag 'In the name of God, to free meetings, free speech and every man a vote'. (KMC)

Broadfield Mills, Lockwood, was built in 1822 by a Mr Berry. Enlarged in 1844, with extra office accommodation added in 1894, it was shared by Gledhill Bros & Co and Kaye and Stewart Ltd. In 1918 the King and Queen visited Kaye and Stewart, which continued to expand and modernise over the years. But by 1976 production had been moved to an associate company at Rashcliffe. In 1902 (some records claim 1905) the managers of Kaye and Stewart arranged for an extensive photographic record of the mills to be taken, from a general view of the mills in Lockwood to the many stages involved in the production through to the dispatch of the finished cloth.   (M/0068)

The *Examiner* ran a series on the textile industry in 1954 and, although half a century later, the processes used in 1902 had not changed greatly. All the machinery in Broadfield Mills was powered by steam engines, this one in the 'new' mill.   (M/0052)

When the fleece arrived at the mill first it was cleaned or scoured. The wool was carded and condensed into a number of threads to be wound on to the bobbins. These threads are then combined into one thread in the spinning process. For worsted the thread successively goes through the processes of drawing, roving, spinning and twisting before the winding takes place, creating a thread in which the fibres are laid parallel. This photograph shows the roving boxes or roving frames at Broadfield Mills.   (M/0069)

In the spinning process for woollens the fibres cross and recross. Therefore combing, drawing and spinning were necessary. Whereas one person used a single spinning wheel the invention of the Spinning Jenny meant that one person could control several spindles at once. Spinning and drawing at Broadfield Mills 1902.   (M/0076)

After spinning there are various other processes, such as winding, and warping before the wool can be made into cloth. On the loom there is a combination of a number of parallel threads, the warp, with a thread inserted between them at right angles, alternately under and over the warp, known as the weft. These weaving machines were in the old weaving shed at Broadfield Mills.   (M/0012)

Once woven, the material was mended to repair any small flaws and broken threads. Although the wool could be dyed at any stage it was often dyed as a piece. Other finishing processes, depending on the type of woollen being produced, would include fulling, tentering and cropping. The dye-house at Broadfield Mills in 1902.   (M/0071)

The invention of the Jacquard loom meant that it was much easier to weave the fancy patterns that were so much in demand in the 19th century. Today such looms are still in use often for the design of fabric before it is set up on the much faster modern machinery.

(M/0053)

The fabric was then passed to the packing room to be sent out to its destination, which in the case of many Huddersfield woollens could have been anywhere in the world.
(M/0057)

In 1972 Gledhill Brothers of Broadfield Mills received the 30,000th Swiss made Sultzer weaving machine. It was the first machine of its type to be installed in England. Mr R.Leutert, a director of Sultzer, presented a golden shuttle to Mr Frank Hanson of Gledhills to commemorate the occasion.
(Ex72.1983)

Moxon's of Kirkburton opened Southfield Mills, a light and airy building in 1950. Started in 1948 the completed mill was designed so that all the processes followed each other in a logical order to produce a fine worsted fabric for export and the high-class home market. In 1973 The *Examiner* reported that a special cloth woven and named appropriately 'Moxon's End of the Rainbow' had proved very popular with shoppers at one of Japan's largest department stores.   (Ex50.11941)

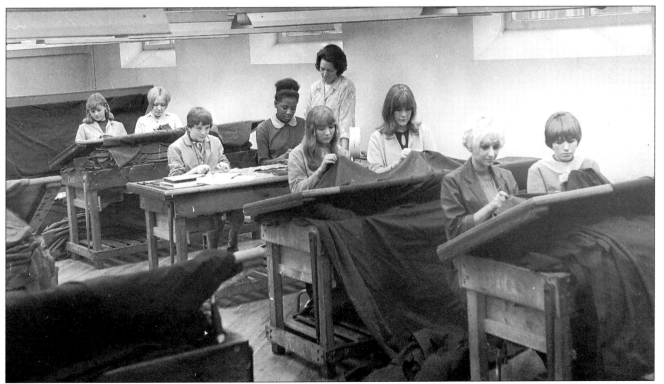

In October 1968 G.Mallinson Ltd of Spring Grove Mills, Linthwaite opened a 'school' to train menders. Girls were tested for eyesight and taught the skills of mending in a programme that conformed with the requirements of the Industrial Training Act. Previously girls had to 'pay' to learn. The *Examiner* commented that it was 'a clear indication of the high value which Colne Valley firms attach to the training of youngsters for a department which is most important to every manufacturer of worsted cloth'.   (Ex68.5008)

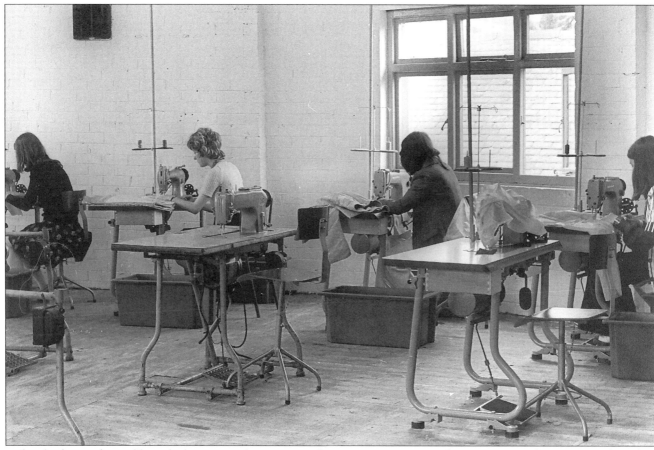

'A bright future for Kiddies clothing' was the report in the *Examiner* in 1973 about an empty factory at Golcar that had been taken by Leonard Hicks to produce clothes specially designed for children. (Ex.73.5180)

Fire is one of the greatest hazards for mills, the grease in the wool permeates the building, making it very flammable. In March 1971 a serious fire destroyed the warehouse at Bath Mills, Lockwood causing over £50,000 worth of damage. Over 20 men were evacuated as firemen tried to bring the blaze under control. (Ex71.1722)

Changes in technology has made many mill buildings redundant. Rock Mills, established in 1879 by Joseph Sykes & Co Ltd, was closed in March 1970 with the loss of some 200 jobs. Hundreds watched as the mill chimney was demolished on a Sunday morning in February 1975. (Ex75.1387)

One of Huddersfield's most important engineering concerns was founded by David Brown in Vulcan Street, Huddersfield. After several moves the firm arrived at Park Works, Lockwood in 1918. The family had owned Park Cottage since the turn of century and Sir David Brown, chairman for many years, was born there in 1904. Originally most of the work was the manufacture of gears for textile industry, but after World War One included motor engines and ships for the Admiralty. In 1949 they started to build Aston Martin and Lagonda cars. By 1977 they were concentrating on the making of gears again. (SC/484)

Tractors were produced by David Brown's in 1933. They set up a new company David Brown Tractors to produce the tractors and a new marketing division, Harry Ferguson Ltd to sell them. The tractor production moved out to Meltham Mills in 1939. These tractors were exported all over the world, but many local farmers also employed them in their daily work on the farm as here on Castle Hill in the 1960s.   (HLSA)

Brook Motors was founded in 1904 in Threadneedle Street by Ernest Brook, moved to Empress Works, St Thomas's Road, and extended to Hope Bank, Honley in 1956. Shell and tank parts were made in World War One and radar and parts of Rolls-Royce Merlin engines in World War Two. Miss Valerie Smith was the works queen in January 1955. The company is now called Brook Crompton Parkinson Motors (Brook Motors Ltd).   (Ex54.5812)

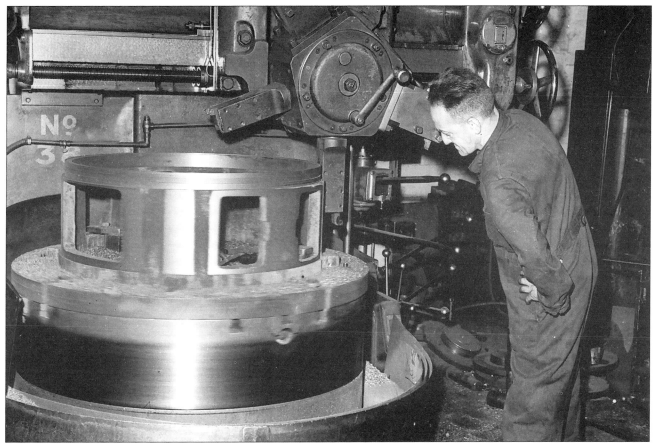

Thomas Broadbent & Sons Ltd was founded in 1864 due to the development of the steam engine. In 1934 they had manufactured the bridge opening gear for the Tees Bridge at Middlesbrough. In February 1955 Harold Brook was using a vertical bore in the light machine shop, just one of the many processes carried out in the company's building.
(Ex55.220)

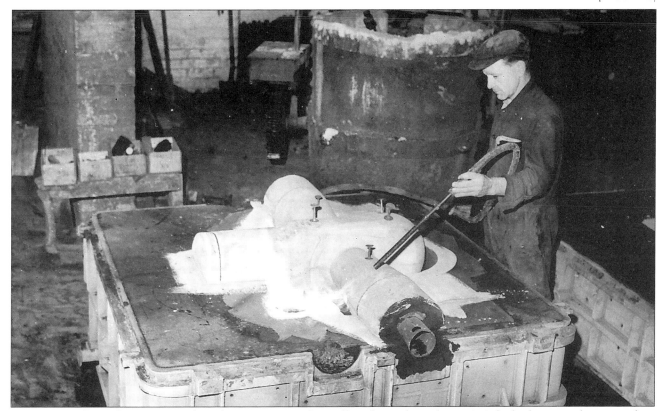

In 1834 Joseph Hopkinson started working in Spring Place off Lockwood Road. By 1852, he had patented a new safety valve for steam engines. The firm moved to Birkby in 1904 making valves for engines and mini submarines during World War Two. Now noted for making high pressure valves for such as power stations throughout the world. In 1955 the steel foundry was reported as being one of the busiest departments where a variety of steel work took place. Mr John O'Connor is seen working on a mould for a valve body.
(Ex54.5928)

W.C. Holmes & Co Ltd at Turnbridge were involved in the manufacture of gas making plants when this photograph of Mr S.Briggs was published in the *Examiner* in February 1955. The company later merged to become Peabody Holmes.

(Ex55.110)

Yet another of the light engineering companies in Huddersfield is the Highfield Gear and Engineering Co. Originally started at Highfields where they cut complete gears and cut teeth in customer's blanks. They moved to the Karrier Works in 1936. Mr J.C.Daley was photographed by the *Examiner* at work on one of the battery of bevel gear generators in 1955.

(Ex55.900)

Sykes and Sugden Ltd of George Street, a firm of electrical engineers branched out and made a motor car in 1919. A three-wheeler car, it was known as the LSD. Later moving to Linthwaite, the company eventually made about 600 cars that cost between £146 and £161. A 1921 Standard model is on display in Tolson Museum.   (KMC)

In 1856 Read Holliday started the production of the magenta dye for sale to the local textile industry. One hundred years later the huge Dalton ICI (now Zeneca) site produced a wide range of organic chemicals and was the most up-to-date in the world. This aerial photograph shows the size of the Dalton site in 1993.   (Ex3623-33a-93)

Heavy industry has always been seen as a male preserve but in 1974, the men 'made way' for Miss Agnes Grieve who was made an honorary member of the works Foreman's Association. The manager in charge of central training at ICI Huddersfield, Miss Grieve said that she was used to being the only woman in most aspects of her work.

(Ex74.3804)

Messrs Peter Conacher & Co Ltd were established in Huddersfield in 1854. Peter Conacher had been sent to Huddersfield to erect an organ at Highfield Congregational Church. He was so impressed with the musical knowledge of the people of the town that he decided to set up on his own. The business started in George Street (*see* page 35) but moved to Springwood. A high degree of skill and care is needed in the production of organs and Mr Percy Goodson was photographed at work making a 4ft diapason.

(Ex55.5429)

Hepworth Iron Company Ltd was founded in 1858 by successful cotton manufacturers as an iron works. In 1868 they started to make sanitary pipes, blue engineering bricks and fire bricks. Work was in progress in the jointing department as the pipes were placed on a conveyer belt for passage through the department. (Ex55.0429)

In 1955 Hepworth's were described as having up-to-date pipe manufacturing and engineering plants, a coal mine, a gas manufacturing plant and, prior to 1953, they had even generated their own electricity. Mr Gordon Hampshire was the driver of 'Ebor', one of the company's two engines that operated on the two miles of track leading to the main line. (Ex55.0430)

Coal has been mined in the Huddersfield area since mediaeval times and in the 14th century there were day eyes or bellpits. Pits as we know them today developed in the 19th century. The only pit in this area still open is the Mining Museum based at Caphouse Colliery. Denby Dale Colliery photographed in about 1900.   (0054/938)

In November 1972 it was announced that Shuttle Eye Colliery at Grange Moor was to close. The shock announcement claimed that reserves of coal had been exhausted. As the only pit still using the traditional hand hewing methods to cut the coal, the report said that it had a higher than the national average for production at 45cwt per man shift.   (Ex72.7952)

Miners arrive at the surface after their last shift as Shuttle Eye Colliery closed on 27 April 1973 having run out of coal. 'Everyone worked for everyone else, and we had lots of fun' said Bernard Newburn who had worked at Shuttle Eye for 12 years, 'but now it's over' read the *Examiner* headline. According to legend the pit got its name from a textile worker who lost an eye because of a flying shuttle and took up mining instead. (Ex73.2751)

Stone is the traditional building material in the area but bricks have played their part. In the early years of the 20th century these men worked at the John Walker's brickworks in Linthwaite.   (0054/1914)

There has always been a demand for drink of various types and in the Huddersfield area we are fortunate in having a good water supply suitable for the manufacture of beer and soft drinks. In the 19th century most manufacturers had ornate bill headings and this of George Armitage Haigh of Honley is no exception.   (0054/1073)

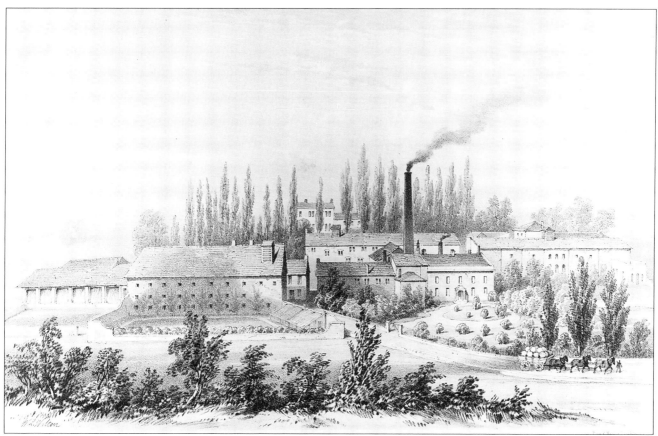

Lockwood Brewery made use of the good water in the River Holme. It was the first brewery to use the Yorkshire stone square system of fermentation which was developed by Dr Priestley. The site was developed by Timothy Bentley and used for the production of beer until 1962 when it was taken over by Bass Charrington.   (HLSA)

In April 1871 Ben Shaw trundled his flat-bottomed wheelbarrow to make his first delivery of his 'non-alcoholic beverage' to Thornton's Temperance Hotel. From such small roots the company extended to build the purposee-built mineral water factory in Willow Lane, Birkby which can be seen in the background of this 1978 drawing. Today the company produces a wide range of products and exports all over the world from its factories at Birkby and Honley.

(Illustration courtesy of Ben Shaw's)

In 1996 the *Examiner* celebrated its 125th anniversary as a daily publication. Founded in 1871 the paper would have been set by hand from cases of loose type. By 1905 the Linotype machines were used to set slugs of type, a line at a time, that were then made up by hand into pages.   (Ex924-11-96)

The original printing press used by the *Examiner* was a four-feeder flatbed from Messrs. Dawson of Otley which produced 2,000 copies an hour. Purchased in 1924 this Crabtree press served the *Examiner* for 41 years and produced 25,000 copies an hour.   (Ex923-15-96)

The *Examiner* was at the forefront of modernisation when the printing section moved to Aspley and a Rockwell Tribune press was installed. The huge rolls of paper await their turn to pass through the printing press.

(Ex.AOUT 1255-24-94)

The various pages of the Examiner run through the press to be cut, folded and checked ready for distribution to local newsagents. (Ex.AOUT 1255-22-94)

Once the printing presses had moved to Aspley, the old building in Ramsden Street was no longer essential and was not an ideal home for the new technology, such as Apple Macintosh computers, that were being introduced. Therefore the *Examiner* editorial offices were moved to purpose-built premises in Queen Street South, maintaining a presence in the town centre with a new public office on the corner of Market Street and Cloth Hall Street. (Ex461-96)

Huddersfield's Transport

There are remains of many ancient routes in the Huddersfield area, ranging from the Roman Road at Marsden and Slack, to the Monastic Ways such as the one which crossed the River Colne at Colne Bridge. Causeways or causeys, such as this at Marsden, were stone paths raised above the level of the ground, originally for the pack horses that crossed the countryside, some later became footpaths on the edge of the road, others remain crossing the fields between villages. (Ex73.5088)

Hey Green Bridge over the River Colne at Marsden is one of the few surviving pack-horse bridges on the route over the Pennines. In the days before there were good roads or canals all produce was carried by pack horse or on the rivers. (M/0196)

In the 18th century conditions on many roads had deteriorated and new developments in transport meant that improvements were essential. Turnpike Trusts were set up to build new roads and they recouped the cost by charging tolls at Toll Houses or Toll Bars like this one at Bradley. In the Huddersfield area there were the Wakefield and Austerlands Turnpike opened in 1759; Dewsbury to Elland via Bradley Lane; Huddersfield to Halifax via Grimescar, designed and built by `Blind Jack' Metcalf in 1777; and Leeds Road to Cooper Bridge, as part of route from Leeds to Manchester. (RH3/27A)

Road repairs have been increasingly mechanised. This road roller was used in Shepley in the early 1900s. (TM/6B)

For many local people in 1969 the building of the M62 became a Sunday afternoon outing. They would drive out to watch the progress and wonder at the huge machines that were being used in its construction.   (Ex69.4806)

Opened in 1970, the M62 crosses the Pennines from Yorkshire into Lancashire. At Scammonden it includes this spectacular bridge. The rock taken from the cutting was used to build the dam over which the road passes.

(Ex74.2493)

One of the hazards of modern traffic is the difficulty pedestrians have in crossing busy roads. The students at Huddersfield Polytechnic blocked traffic on Queensgate in November 1972 demanding a footbridge to the Market Hall and thence to the town centre. A Pelican crossing was installed but in 1995 plans were again proposed for a spectacular footbridge to join the University to the town centre. (Ex72.7620)

The Huddersfield Narrow Canal was built between 1794 and 1811. Designed by Robert Outram, the coming of the railway in the 1840s put the canal into decline. The canal was bought by the railway companies who used it to take away the spoil as they drove new tunnels through the Pennines at Standedge. The navvies who worked on the construction of a double tunnel in 1890 lived in these huts. (M/0195)

The settlement of Tunnel End at Marsden developed as a result of the canal and railway tunnels through the Pennines. The use of the canal declined and by 1974 it was in serious decay. The Huddersfield Narrow Canal Society was formed to restore the canal and many locks have now been reopened. Plans are being made to reopen the Stand-edge Tunnel.

(Ex74.352)

As part of the restoration work on the Ramsden Canal various locks have been rebuilt. This lock at Red Doles was emptied and rebuilt in October 1980. (Ex80.10140)

The railway arrived in Huddersfield in 1847 when the LNWR opened Huddersfield Station. The network extended to serve the Colne and Holme Valleys with branch lines to Meltham, Holmfirth, Clayton West, and Kirkburton. In 1996 the two surviving lines connect Huddersfield with Leeds, Wakefield and Manchester, and the Penistone Line to Sheffield. Brockholes Station in the early 1900s was typical of the many village stations. (120/41810)

The *Flying Scotsman* made a short stop in Huddersfield in September 1968 at a time when steam was being replaced by the diesel units. One railway enthusiast, Mr Rogers Whittaker, had flown all the way from New York just to ride on the train. (Ex68.3965)

Huddersfield Corporation introduced the first municipal transport service in Britain when the first steam tram made its way from Fartown to Lockwood in January 1883. An example of a steam tram can be seen in St George's Square (on page 38). Electric trams were introduced in 1901. The original routes still form the basis of the bus system today. They covered areas of the town and up the valleys as far as Honley and Slaithwaite. This electric tram was photographed at the terminus in Honley.   (0054/750)

Tramcars No.69 and No.54 travel along Queen Street South to Newsome in the 1930s. Bates & Co. (Huddersfield) Ltd, woollen yarn spinners, occupy the buildings to the right, the new *Examiner* offices now occupy a site to the left of this picture.   (WBS/35)

Westgate in full celebratory dress as Huddersfield rejoices in the coronation of King George V in June 1911. The electric tram car No.29 is making its way to Lindley. (WS/1598)

Electric trams were replaced by trolley buses in 1933. These quiet electric buses were suited to the steep hillsides that many of our roads climb. By January 1939 the system had reached Longwood. The Longwood service was opened by this trolley bus which turned round to return through the town centre to Sheepridge. The last trolley bus ran from Westgate to Waterloo and Outlane on Saturday, 13 July 1968.   (WBS/17)

The march of progress meant that trolley buses were considered too expensive to run and so motor buses were ordered. In an attempt to reduce costs 'one man' buses were introduced, making conductors redundant. The first one-man double deck bus ran on the Almondbury route in March 1970. It was felt by many passengers that it took more time to board the bus making the journey longer.

(Ex70.1104)

Poorhouse to the National Health Service

Huddersfield appointed John Benson Pritchett as its first Medical Officer in 1873. His reports show how he fought overcrowded homes, lack of sanitation and his belief in the value of fresh air, clean water and the proper care of mothers and children. The importance of clean, accessible water was not neglected and over the 19th and 20th centuries new reservoirs have been opened such as at Digley where in February 1974 water was flooding over the spillway for the first time in four years. The height of the reservoir had risen by four feet and the incessant roar of the overflow could be heard in the waterman's cottage nearby.   (0054/0955)

Prior to the opening in Pack Horse Yard of the Huddersfield Dispensary in July 1812 there were no hospital services and very little medical care in the Huddersfield area. There were a few doctors but they were expensive and most people would use the services of 'bonesetters' or 'quacks' such as Richard Horsfall, known as 'Merrydale Dick'.   (KMC)

The Huddersfield Royal Infirmary opened in 1831 to care for 'the reception of a limited number of In-Patients; more especially for those frequent Accidents arising from the extensive Use of Machinery'. Financed by local businessmen it was built on New North Road and is seen here in 1895.   (RH6/12c)

Matron and Sister ruled the wards, but the nurses tried to make them as comfortable as possible. At first there was little the doctors and nurses could do to cure a patient, because of the lack of medical knowledge. Ward 2 at the Huddersfield Royal Infirmary in the 1890s.   (M/0113)

Huddersfield Royal Infirmary moved to its new site in Oakes in the 1970s. One feature of its service made headline news in 1974 when a conveyer belt system was introduced for the serving of patients' meals. Designed to improve choice and ensure that food was hot when it arrived on the wards. (Ex74.7318)

The Crosland Moor Workhouse that opened in 1872 consisted of a vagrants ward, an infirmary and a school, 'removing from the community those who could not support themselves'. A Poor Law Institute by 1913, it was renamed St Luke's Hospital in 1931, and transferred to public use in 1934. The Ministry of Health announced a £1.25m scheme to redevelop St Luke's Hospital in 1962, practically all of the original Workhouse disappeared and it was to become the town's second hospital. (KCS)

Over the years medical knowledge has increased, and the *Examiner* celebrated such a triumph when baby Christopher Stynes went home in July 1972. Weighing just 1lb 11oz when he was born, he was able to leave the Special Baby Care Unit ten weeks later to make his acquaintance with his sister Joanne. (Ex72.4079)

Storthes Hall, built in 1791, was converted to a 'School for Mentally Defective Children of the West Riding County Council' at the start of 20th century. Extended between 1902 and 1918, at its peak, the psychiatric hospital was the home of over 2,000 patients in the care of over 1,000 staff. In an attempt to help patients to lead a normal life several shops were opened in November 1974 including this grocery shop and a boutique from where patients could buy their own clothes.   (Ex74.8258)

The Storthes Hall Hospital was closed in 1992. The site was photographed from the air in 1994 as it awaited conversion to its new role as the Storthes Hall Campus of Huddersfield University.   (Ex4338-16a-94)

Half-timer to University Days

Education was only available to the wealthy, but many local philanthropists left money to found schools. One example is the Almondbury Grammar School which developed from a Chantry School and received a Charter in 1608. (SC/0002)

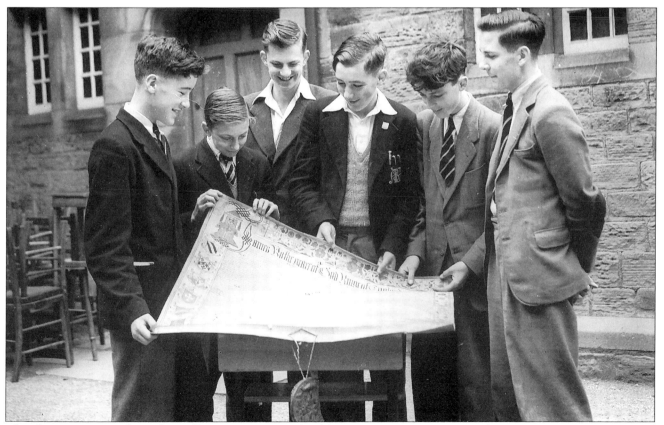

The charter presented to Almondbury Grammar School by King James was missing for many years. It was spotted by a group of boys visiting an exhibition staged by the Yorkshire Archaeological Society in July 1952. From left to right Michael Fawcett, David Anderson, Thomas A.Blackburn, John Earnshaw, Allan Dobson and Alan E.Sykes with the charter that they found. (Ex52.2743)

In the lead up to the 1870 Education Act the Taunton Commission surveyed all the schools in the Huddersfield area. Outside the County Borough, Longwood Grammar School in 1868, had 39 pupils of whom 27 paid fees of sixpence a week.
(0054/1082)

The Collegiate School, a Church of England School founded in 1838, was one of the two proprietary schools in Huddersfield to provide secondary education. Increasing financial difficulties led to it joining with the Huddersfield College in 1885.
(RH3/57D)

Huddersfield College was also founded in 1838 but served the wealthy nonconformist families of the town. In 1868 the Taunton Commission declared that there was little difference between it and the Collegiate, except size. In 1958 the school, and Hillhouse Secondary, moved to become the Huddersfield New College in new buildings at Salendine Nook. (M/0306)

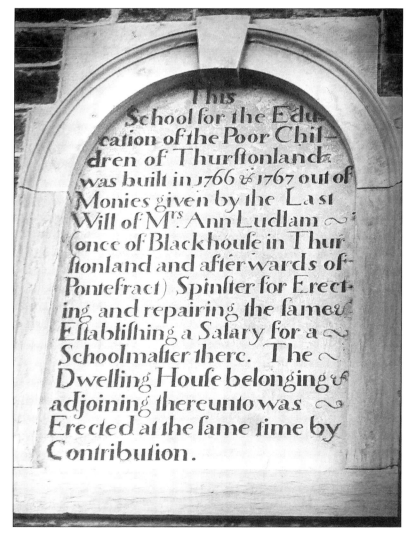

Many of the villages surrounding Huddersfield provided a basic education for the children. This plaque was photographed on the school buildings in Thurstonland in 1972. (Ex72.2951)

School photographs are not a new phenomena, this Mount Pleasant school class faced a long wait for the cameraman in about 1908. In 1870 the Education Act allowed School Boards to insist that children between five and 13 must attend school. As a concession children over ten were allowed to work and attend school halftime.   (120/337-2)

Post-war Britain has built on the foundations laid by the early educational pioneers. Pre-school education in the form of nurseries played an important role in the war effort. Their popularity continued afterwards and by March 1970 Milnsbridge Nursery School was 'catering for all in need since more women were going out to work'. There were three day nurseries in Huddersfield with another planned on Cambridge Road. Nurse Metcalfe is seen playing with four happy youngsters at Milnsbridge Nursery School.   (Ex70.1426)

There were not sufficient places at Nursery School for all children therefore many mothers sent their children to the local playgroup. The National Pre-school Playgroups Week in May 1969 was featured in the *Examiner* when a reporter visited a selection of playgroups including Lindley Methodist Pre-School Playgroup. Mrs Anne Senior, of Birchencliffe, is seen showing her young son Richard what he had to look forward to when he joined his sister at Lindley Playgroup. (Ex69.2188)

Then came the important day, the first day at 'proper' school. Most years the *Examiner* has recorded this important day and in September 1972 visited Birkby Infants School and photographed Ian Meike and commented that 'Tying shoelaces is a job for any chap on his first day at school'.

(Ex72.5267)

Children at Scammonden were forced to abandon their village school when it was in danger of slipping into the new Scammonden Reservoir in 1970. The school was founded in 1824 but the building which dated from the 1860s, had recently been improved. The children would have to travel to Barkisland or Outlane for their primary education. Mrs Joan Busfield and her assistant Mrs Janet Davis are with the children pointing their way forward.   (Ex70.1551)

Children from St Joseph's RC Junior School enjoy a history lesson at the Colne Valley Museum in 1981. (Ex81.1328)

Looking smart in their shorts and blazers, these boys from Hillhouse Secondary School had been to Ramsden Street Baths when their photograph was taken in November 1956. (Ex56.5256)

The division between lessons for boys and girls was challenged in the 1970s. In 1972 the boys of Skelmanthorpe Secondary Modern School were being taught to cook in domestic science lessons taught by Mrs Sheila Westerby.

(Ex72.6132)

The 1970s brought many changes to education in Huddersfield. The grammar schools were abolished, secondary schools became High Schools, Greenhead and New College became Sixth Form Colleges. Greenhead had always been a girls school but in 1974 these three new boys made 'quick work of getting to know the girls'.   (Ex73.8980)

Almondbury Grammar School became King James's College and accepted the first girls into the sixth form in 1974. Since then it has become a High School. The headmaster Mr J.A.Conley (back left) and the deputy head, Mr A.D.Bush (back right) and boys from King James's welcome the girls, who are (from the left) June Bayling, Linda Taylor, Danielle Galvin, Mandy Brawn, Linda Hepplestone and Maria Lijke.   (Ex74.5694)

Higher education in Huddersfield has developed from the early days of the Mechanics Institution which was founded in 1825. This fine building was erected in 1882 as the Huddersfield Technical School and Mechanic's Institution in Queen Street South. Designed by Edward Hughes the building was opened by the Duke of Somerset in 1883.
(GH2/12A)

The Huddersfield Technical College became a Polytechnic in 1970, although the name passed to a new Technical College housed in the empty Huddersfield Infirmary buildings. By 1994 the Polytechnic had become a University. This photograph shows the Central Services Building which was opened by HRH the Duchess of Kent in May 1977.
(ExCV3)

The expansion of the University of Huddersfield has led to a shortage of accommodation, not only for student halls of residence but for the various faculties. The closing down of large institutions and 'Care in the Community' meant that the former Storthes Hall Hospital site was available. The first students to occupy the first phase of the development on the Storthes Hall site moved in during the autumn of 1995.
(Ex96.90-11a)

Many people live to enjoy a full and active retirement. Mrs Edith Bentley founded the Huddersfield Owls (Over 50s Weekday Leisure Group) in 1983 and in 1985 the Huddersfield Branch of the University of the Third Age which, in 1996, is the largest in the UK. In May 1993 she was honoured by a civic 'thank you' from the Mayor of Kirklees, Councillor David Wright. (Ex3278-16A-93)

A Huddersfield educationalist, Brian Jackson, was instrumental in the setting up of the Open University, and in recommending that there should be a Ministry for Children. He was involved in the National Children's centre at Longroyd Bridge and following his untimely death was honoured by the naming of the new National Children's Centre as the Brian Jackson Centre in the railway warehouses on New North Parade. Brian Jackson is seen playing with his children in 1974. (Ex74.5758)

Civic Pride, Community and Culture

The Letters Patent for the sale of the Manor of Huddersfield by Queen Elizabeth I in 1599 and the Charter granting market rights to the Ramsden family had been missing for many years but a surprise letter offered them for sale to Huddersfield Council. Councillor Clifford Stephenson, chairman of the Estates and Property Management Committee oversaw the purchase and in 1970 displayed them to Council members at a dinner celebrating the purchase of the Ramsden Estate by the Corporation in 1920 for £800,000. (Ex70.5880)

Over the years only 29 people have been made Freemen of Huddersfield as well as the Duke of Wellington's Regiment and the Huddersfield Choral Society. The last Freemen to be appointed included Viscount Montgomery, Harold Wilson, and three councillors, Alderman D.Graham, Alderman Clifford Stephenson and Alderman H.Hartley in March 1973. From left to right: Alderman H.Hartley, the Mayor Alderman W.Eric Whitaker, Harold Wilson, Alderman C.Stephenson and Alderman D.Graham. (Ex73.1429)

The Armorial Ensigns
and Standard of the
BOROUGH OF KIRKLEES

College of Arms
London. May 1974.

Richmond Herald of A

When the new Kirklees Metropolitan Council came into being a new Coat of Arms was designed by the Borough Herald, and approved by the College of Heralds in 1974.   (Ex74.3488)

Councillor John Mernagh was the last representative of 106 years of civic pride when he was elected as the last Mayor of Huddersfield in May 1973. A period of great civic pride as all the changes in the town centre had opened or were about to be opened such as the Sports Centre, Welfare Centre and new Market Hall.   (Ex73.3365)

The Charter of Incorporation of the Kirklees Metropolitan Borough was displayed to the Huddersfield Council meeting in December 1973. County Councillor B.Murphy, Councillor H.Hartley, Councillor T.Meghany and chief executive Me E.Dixon are seen looking at the new charter.   (Ex73.11487)

The first Mayor of Kirklees, Councillor Reginald Hartley was invested with his chain of office in a ceremony at Huddersfield Town Hall on 6 April 1974. In his speech he referred to the 'difficult and challenging year ahead for local government' as Huddersfield joined in the eighth largest authority in the country with boundaries stretching from Batley to Marsden. (Ex74.1989)

In July 1970 Princess Margaret came to open the Welfare Centre, calling in at the Town Hall and the new Market Hall *en route*. There were red faces at the Town Hall when her car arrived 12 minutes early and they were not ready to greet her with the red carpet welcome. (Ex70.4109)

Civic dignitaries, Mayors and Mayoresses have visited many of the Council's homes and services over the years. At Christmas 1968 the Mayor and Mayoress Alderman T.Cliffe and Councillor Mrs S.Cliffe visited the children at All Saints Home in Almondbury as well as homes at Fernside, Haigh House (Bradley) and Fartown Grange. (Ex68.8046)

Huddersfield has always been fortunate in the quality of the people who serve in public life and the many thousands that serve in voluntary capacities, running services for the less fortunate and raising funds for a wide variety of charitable causes. The following photographs show just a few of the many people and the causes they serve. The Huddersfield Common Good Trust is just one of many that make grants to Huddersfield Groups and in 1972 made its largest grant to date to the Huddersfield Society for the Mentally Handicapped to improve facilities at Waverley Hall. The children and young people who used the Hall really appreciated the changes. (Ex72.2628)

There are many ways of raising funds for charity such as the Huddersfield Ladies Lifeboat Luncheon Club who over the years have supported the work of the Royal National Lifeboat Institution. At their annual meeting in May 1973 Mrs Olga Arnold presented Mrs L.M.Beech with the chain of office.   (Ex73.2848)

Miss Joan Donnelly worked tirelessly to raise funds for Guide Dogs for the Blind, going into the schools with her own Guide Dogs and attending many fund-raising activities. In spite of her own handicap she was always ready to help others. Unfortunately she died in 1995 and will be much missed.   (Ex74.178)

Huddersfield people have always tended to help themselves when they have difficulties. The Huddersfield Gingerbread Group for single-parent families used yet another of the popular fund-raising activities. They asked the MP for Huddersfield East to open their Christmas Fayre held in the Drill Hall in December 1973. From the left; Mrs D.North, J.P.W.Mallalieu MP, Justine North, Mrs C.Turner and Mrs S.Stead. (Ex73.11427)

Not content with celebrating 200 years of services at Highfield Congregational Chapel in 1972 the congregation decided to do something for the town and presented a new Meals on Wheels Van to the Huddersfield Women's Royal Voluntary Service. From the left: Mrs Kathleen Thaw, Mrs Wendy Sugden, Mrs Molly Lewis following the presentation of the keys discuss the meals with Mrs Gwen Pearson and Mrs Norah Davidson (the County Borough Organiser of WRVS). (Ex72.2120)

Young people have a wide range of activities open to them in the Huddersfield area, including youth clubs and the uniformed organisations such as Scouts, Guides, Boys Brigade and Sea, Army and Air Cadet Corps. The Air Training Corps paraded through the town centre when they moved to their new headquarters at the Drill Hall on Sunday, 4 October 1970.   (Ex70.6047)

Huddersfield is noted for its musical activities. The Huddersfield Choral Society may be the best known but there are many other choirs, orchestras and bands throughout the area. As representatives, the following few have been chosen. The Methodist Choir holds regular concerts in the Town Hall as does the Choral Society. Their Christmas concert is just as popular and in 1969 they were fortunate to premiere a new carol specially written for them. Accompanied by Lindley Brass Band they sang *As Joseph was A'Walking* to a tune written by choir member J.H.Marsden.   (Ex69.9065)

A smaller group, the Glee and Madrigal Society was about to hold a Victorian evening in the Town Hall when this photograph was taken in 1974. The Glee and Madrigal Group changed its name to the Huddersfield Singers in the 1990s.

(Ex74.7745)

Amateur operatic societies flourish in this area with many local churches and villages having their own society. In February 1972 the Scissett Amateur Operatic Society presented *The Boy Friend* in spite of great difficulties. A time of fuel shortages and scheduled power cuts, the group had a generator waiting to take over when the power was turned off at eight o'clock.   (Ex72.0944)

The music of Gilbert and Sullivan has always been popular and usually receives good reviews in the *Examiner*. In 1972 the Huddersfield and District Gilbert and Sullivan Society produced their version of *HMS Pinafore*. The photograph shows some of the cast members including at the front, Brian Johnson, Elaine Brown and Margaret Armitage, behind them are Roger Mitchell, Humphrey Lewis and George Shaw. (Ex72.2560)

There are two important competitive music festivals in the area. The Mrs Sunderland is justly famous as is the Haydn Wood held in the Holme Valley. Jane and Louise England were winners in Class 3 piano duet (9/11 years) at the Haydn Wood Festival held in October 1973. (Ex73.10477)

Huddersfield's stage presentations must not be neglected with many drama groups from the Thespians to local village and church groups and the regular school plays. In 1994 the new Lawrence Batley Theatre was opened in what was originally the Queen Street Mission. With state of the art technology, two theatres and sufficient back up space for rehearsals and all the other things needed for a show, the theatre has proved very successful with both audiences and groups in the town. (c95 0504 2/12)

Huddersfield Town AFC have always enjoyed a good following. The Leeds Road ground has attracted big crowds, travelling by these electric trams before they were replaced in 1933. (WBS5/3)

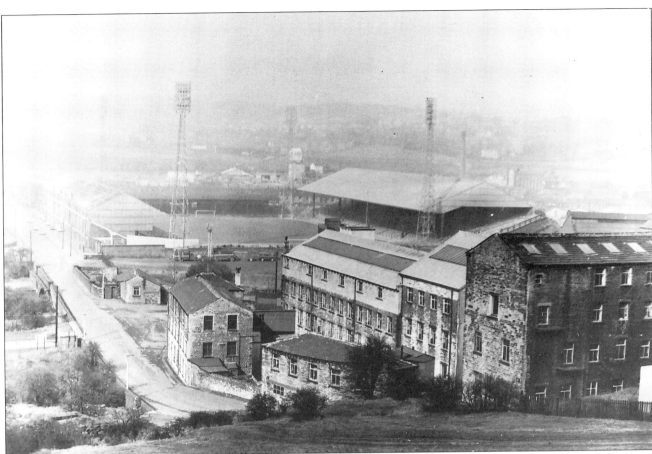

Taken from Kilner Bank, the lighting towers dominate this view of Huddersfield Town's football ground in 1964. This ground was demolished in 1995 and replaced with the new McAlpine Stadium.   (HLSA)

Huddersfield Town AFC celebrated their fine new stadium by moving up into the First Division of the Football League. The new Kirklees Stadium, as it was originally known, was sponsored by many people including Lawrence Batley and Sir Alfred McAlpine.   (c94 11 09-31a)

Designed as the home of Huddersfield Town, the stadium also hosts the Huddersfield Giants Rugby League Club and a wide range of events that can range from pop and classical concerts to large rallies and promotions. In 1995 it won the prestigious Building of the Year Award from the Royal Institute of British Architects.   (c95 05 09-48)

Many other sports are popular in the Huddersfield area, ranging from the small local football clubs such as the successful Emley side, seen here playing against Farsley Celtic in December 1973. According to the *Examiner*, 'the ball eluded Emley striker S.B.Greaves and the Farsley defender in this duel on the snow-covered pitch' as Emley won through to the third round of the Yorkshire League Cup.   (Ex73.11293)

Lascelles Hall is one of the more successful local cricket clubs which has sent players on to the Yorkshire county team. In September 1972 they played against Kirkburton at home. Kirkburton won this game to become the Huddersfield District League Champions, winning the Byram Shield.   (Ex72.6174)

Gymnastics became very popular among young people, especially girls, following Olga Korbutt's successes in the Olympic Games. In 1973 there was a waiting list at the Greenhead Gymnastics Club but these girls were lucky members. From the left are Gillian Bailey, Ursula Moran, Janice Wilkinson, Dianne Lovett and Angela Martin.
(Ex73.3074)

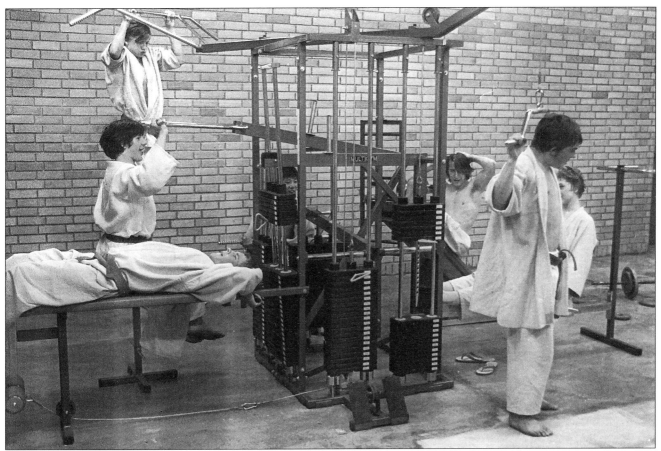

In July 1973 the *Examiner* sent two of their reporters to try out as many sports as they could in one day at the newly opened Huddersfield Sports Centre. Here Bill Knight and Roger Inman join other Centre users as they are put to the 'rack' on what looks like an ancient torture machine but cost £1,000 and was used for weight lifting.   (Ex73.4014)

Her Majesty Queen Elizabeth II visited Huddersfield to open the M62 and Scammonden Water in 1971. Huddersfield's most modern reservoir, it was designed with leisure in mind, with car parks, signed walks and the Scammonden Water Sailing Club. Since then a Scout Activity Centre has also been opened.   (Ex71.6976)

A cold misty after afternoon, but it provided excellent sailing conditions for the new Scammonden Water Sailing Club when the Mayor of Huddersfield visited them in April 1971 and raced with the chairman of the Colne Valley Council, Councillor Mrs H.Swift.   (Ex71.1837)

Outdoor activities have for many years included the intrepid walkers who brave all types of weather. From the thousands who walk or run the Huddersfield Marathons to the scouts who brave the Masters Hike that takes in all three of the local masts, Pole Moor, Holme Moss and Emley Moor. Bad weather forced over 100 contestants out of the hike in October 1973. These Holme Valley scouts had stopped for refreshments and to check their route over Holme Moss. From the left they are Peter Barker, Andrew Walsh, Kevin Jones and Nigel Goldsmith.   (Ex73.10051)

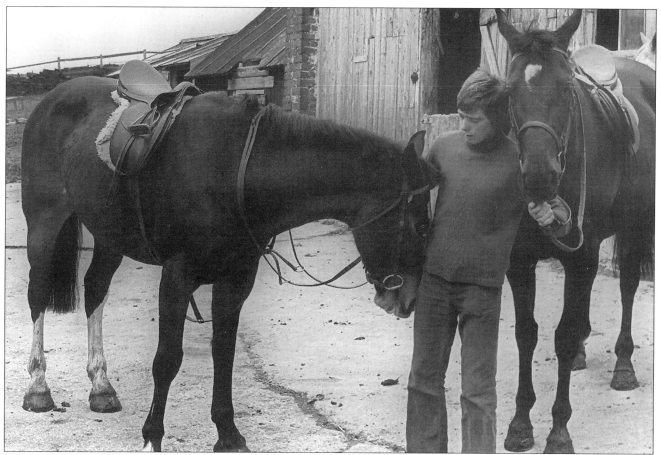

The Whittaker family from Hurst Mount farm in Outlane have been very successful in the world of showjumping. In 1974 John Whittaker was starting out on a career in showjumping looking forward to the chance of representing his country in the Olympic Games. In October 1974 he had recently taken part in helping to win the Nations Cup in the Canadian Junior International Amateur Equestrian Foundation's Horse Show and won £300 as first prize at the Yorkshire Show on Ryan's Son. (Ex74.6924)

The appearance of the Colne Valley Beagles was a sure sign that Autumn had come in October 1973 when they held their opening meet at the Will O'Nats in Meltham. (Ex73.9432)

Right: The traditional 'sings' are not only held at Longwood but in many other areas such as in the Molly Carr Woods on Easter morning and this at Slaithwaite held in May 1969. Hundreds marched through the Slaithwaite town centre in heavy rain to gather in the Market Place for prayers and hymns led by Mr Phillip Holdroyd. The photograph shows Karen and Estelle Clarke and Rachel Pogson as they shelter under their umbrellas.

(Ex69.2270)

Top left: The opening of a whippet racing track at Colne Bridge was recorded in the *Examiner* in 1972. These dogs are about to take part in races there in 1974. (Ex74.6134)

Bottom left: There are many other activities that attract a wide range of followers such as English Country Dancing. Dancers from the Lindley branch of the English Folk Song and Dance Society were chosen to take part in a National Folk Festival to be held in the Royal Albert Hall in 1969. They included Mr & Mrs Keys and Miss June Steel who are seen here with Mr Addington and class leader Mrs K.A. Fawthrop.

(Ex69.554)

Other forms of folk dancing are popular, including the Morris Men who regularly appear on the streets of the area such as these on the Piazza in Huddersfield in July 1978.

(Ex78.4554)

Coronations, royal weddings and other national events have been celebrated over many years by street parties. Over 100 children enjoyed a tea and games as part of the celebrations at Fenay Lea Drive when Prince Charles married Lady Diana Spencer in July 1981.

(Ex81.5954)

A large party was arranged by the Huddersfield Hotel which completely filled Beast Market with happy smiling faces in celebration of the Royal Wedding.

(Ex81.5960)

The Ukrainian community fled Hitler's Germany and the Communist regime to reach freedom in Britain. They introduced a continental flavour to Huddersfield as they held a Gala Day in the Transport Department's Playing Fields at Canker Lane. Visitors joined them from as far away as Scotland and London. This group of dancers show off the colourful national dress in August 1950.

(Ex50.12950)

Huddersfield's cultural life has been enhanced over the years by the many immigrants. The Polish community held a Silver Jubilee event in Huddersfield Town Hall in September 1973. Five-year-old Ewa Goraka, Yashin Dobrycki (8) and six-year-old Yagoda Wtodavayk were among the artists taking part in the 3 hour programme of celebration and entertainment.   (Ex73.9093)

Other immigrant groups have settled in the town, West Indians, Chinese and those from the Indian sub-continent. Our schools have developed a multicultural curriculum that reflects aspects of most of these cultures. In October 1973 the Crosland Moor Infants school held a Community Relations Harvest festival which included Asian, English and West Indian songs.
(Ex73.10132)

One of the first Sikh community to have their wedding photograph in the *Examiner* was recorded in January 1975; 'Coconut shells are the bride's lucky wedding symbols' as Miss Paulo Kaur married Mr Onakar Singh. The bride, formerly a nurse at St Luke's Hospital, wore a red chiffon sari embroidered with golden thread as the ceremony took place in Elmwood Avenue conducted by the Priest of the Sikh Temple, Mr Balwant Singh. (Ex75.992)

The Sikh community opened their new Temple in Prospect Street in 1975. They were joined by dignitaries from other temples and representatives of the local Christian churches and the local council. (Ex75.5537)

The Huddersfield area has been rich over the years with many eccentric characters, Wilf Lunn whose's inventions rival those of Heath Robinson, and Jake Mangle-Worzel who has raised many a laugh often on serious issues. Here Wilf Lunn is opening a Summer Fete at Reinwood Junior School in 1981.   (Ex81.4978)

In 1972 Herbert Thorpe was fighting to say that an Englishman's home is his castle. The 71-year-old had written many slogans on the walls of his garden, without planning permission. He and his landlady Mrs A.Heeley were refusing to pay the fines because he said that they were not advertisements but 'proclamations and denunciations'.

(Ex72.6252)

Heritage Quiz
Do you know where these buildings are?
(all are within the ring road)

1. Fashion and flea markets meet in this once veggie building.

2. A public house at the 'top o'th'town'.

3. Financially a fine Yorkshire building.

4. A 'founding father' once lived on the site of this faddy building.

5. At long last we can see this column again after restoration.

6. A gargoyle, but where do civic pride and music meet?

7. Queen Victoria might not have approved of all that happens here!

8. Wonderful architecture, hidden away from church and rail.

9. Fine gates, recently restored, now lead to some of Kirklees employees.

10. Once upon a time you could buy net for your wedding, now the hardware for the internet.

Bibliography

The *Huddersfield Daily Examiner*
The *Huddersfield Weekly Examiner*

Beach, David T. ed. *Huddersfield Trolleybus Memories* (Huddersfield, 1983)
Beilby, A.R. *Churches and Chapels of Kirklees* (Huddersfield, 1978)
Brook, Roy *Huddersfield Corporation Tramways* (Huddersfield, 1983)
Earnshaw, A *Railways in and around Huddersfield, part I* (Stockport, 1993)
Haigh, E.A.H. *Huddersfield: A Most Handsome Town* (Huddersfield, 1992)
Hinchcliffe, Brian *Huddersfield in the Tramway Era* (Sheffield, 1978)
Hinchliffe, A. *A History of King James' Grammar School Almondbury* (Huddersfield, 1963)
Historic Almondbury: The Village on the Hill (Huddersfield, 1975)
Holmes, D.H. *The Mining and Quarrying Industries in the Huddersfield District* (Huddersfield, 1967)
Minter, G. & E. *Discovering old Huddersfield I* (Huddersfield, 1994)
Minter, G. & E. *Discovering old Huddersfield II* (Huddersfield, 1995)
Shackleton, E. *A Living Inheritance* (Huddersfield, 1988)
Spencer, N. *A Scrapbook of Huddersfield* (Huddersfield, 1990)
'Swinburn' *The Penistone Line* (Huddersfield, 1988)
Varley, W.J. *Castle Hill* (Huddersfield, 1973)
Wyles, David *The Buildings of Huddersfield* (Huddersfield, 1985)

Copies of the above books may be consulted, borrowed or in some cases purchased from Huddersfield Library.

Index

Subscribers

Philip Addy, Maxine Addy
Mrs C P Ainley
Margaret Ainley
Mrs Marjorie Stanhope Allen
Mrs Christine Allison
Mr & Mrs J Allison
Richard Appleyard
Bradley Archer
David U Armitage
Frank & Jean Armitage
Ian Armitage
M G & C M Armitage
A & J Armstrong
Mary Aspinall
Dorothy R Atkinson (Miss)
Mr Raymond Austwick
Mrs Betty S Z Aziz
Peter J W Bailey
Edward Ball
Colin Balmforth
E Douglas Bamforth
Mrs Jean Bamforth
Reverend Dennis Barraclough
Mr & Mrs Paul Bastow
Mrs Emily Bates
Mrs Joan Batley
David Battye
Robert A Battye
Ronald Battye
Herbert G Baxter
Alan J Beadsworth
Kevin Beastall
The Beaumont Arms – Kirkstile, Kirkheaton
Lloyd Beaumont
Roy & Jill Beaumont
Mrs Susan Beaumont
Godfrey Bedford
Mr & Mrs W Beck
E Bellamy
M J & N Bennett
Mr Roy Bentley
Mr Mark Bentman
Mr Ashley J Berry
Mr Christopher R Berry
Mr Roy Berry
Mr S Beveridge
Susan E Billington
Ian B Binns
Mrs Mavis Binns
Phillip J Birmingham
Dr H J Black
David Blackburn
Terry & Shirley Blackburn
Douglas R Blacker
T & I Blakey
Mr & Mrs H Blakeley
Marlene & Stuart Blakey

Martin A Booth
Peter Boothroyd
Sydney Boothroyd
Mr K Bottom
J G Bottomley
Brian Bowden
Barbara Bower
Graeme & Silke Bower
Stanley Boyle
Edith Bradbury
D M Bradley
C D Bramham
Nancy Bray
John Brennan
Peter & Pamela Brierley
Raymond Brierley
George L Briggs
Harold & Winnie Broadbent
Bernard & Ann Brook
Mr Eric Brook
Lesley Ann Brook
Lesley E Brook
Maegan Jo Brook
R Adam Brook
Roger Brook
Miss C E Brown
E D Brown
Mr & Mrs H S Brown
Mr J R Brown
Peter Brown
Mr & Mrs L A Bruce
Ernest T Buckless
Joan Bull
John Bullock
A G & P Burford
Shelley Burgin
Mr D R Burke
Eric H Burnley
Mr Fred Bushill
Paul Butcher
Peter & Pat Butterfield
Sylvia Butterworth
Mrs Gwen P Calverley
Martin Roger Calvert
M Carter
Mr & Mrs P J Carter
Robert A Carter
Jean & Leslie Chadwick
Roy Chadwick
Gerald Chaplin
Miss Fiona Christie
William Clark
Mrs V Claydon
James Melvyn Clayton
Mr & Mrs M Colbeck
D M Coldwell
Kevin Coleman

Sylvia & Tim Collins
Mrs Elsie May Cooper
Hazel M Cooper
A D & N M Copley
Chris Corcoran
Mrs Elizabeth M Craig
Jean & John Craig
Andrew Crossley
David Crowther
Judith Crowther, née Knockton
J Cumiskey
Helen Dack
Mr Douglas A Dagge
Gene Danielson
Margaret Davies
Valerie Davies
Winifred Davies, née Crowther Melnyczuk
Mr Douglas Davison
Mrs Winifred Day
Mr D N Dearnley
Norman Dearnley
Dorothy Denniss
C & J A Dews
Peter Dickinson
W Dignan
Anthony Granville Dixon
Ian M Dixon, Nettleton Hill
Anthony Dodgson
Daisy & Jack Donkersley
John Donnelly
Mrs S A Draper
Robert & Sarah Drummond and Family
Mr & Mrs D Duckett
James S Duckett
P Duckworth
Mr C Duffy
Norman Duffy
Valerie Durham
Donald Ian Dyson
Kenneth Dyson
Vilma Dyson
Mrs D A Eastwood
Mavis & George Eastwood
Mr D R Eaton
Mrs Mary Eccles
Eunice Edwards
Trevor & Colleen Ellis
Graham Evans
Harry & Betty Evans
James & Hilary Ewens
Jean Ewing
Anne Exley
Clive Farrand
J F R Farrow
Brian Firth
George & Joan Firth
Margaret & Brian Firth
Barbara K Foster & Peter R Foster
Malcolm Foster
Andrew Fox
William Fox
George R Flynn
Jeffrey Kneale France

Mrs Mary France
Roger France
Lynn F Free
Mrs R Freeman (Herne)
Terry Fuller
Dr John Galvin
John C Galvin
Shirley & Terry Galvin
Joyce Gannon
Michael Allan Gatenby
David E Gledhill
E Gledhill
Philip Gledhill
Frank Goldthorpe
Arthur Goodyear
William & Anne Gore
Stephen Green
Mrs Margaret Gregory
Sydney Griffiths
Monica Grover
Brian & Jean Hadfield
Alastair J Haigh
Mrs Evelyn Haigh
Frank Haigh
M D Haigh
Robert A Haigh
John R Hall
Mrs Phyllis Hampshaw
Geoffrey & Thelma Hampson
Michael Arthur Hannam
J S & J Hanson
Barbara & Michael Hardcastle
Douglas A Harpin
Jim Harris BA (Hons)
Arnold Harrop
Jean Heap
Malcolm & Jennifer L Heap
David Brian Heaton
Mrs Susan M Heaton
Brian & Denise Hebblethwaite
Mr & Mrs J Hebblethwaite and Family
Gwenda Elizabeth Heeley
Pat Hepworth
David, Linda, Holly & Tom Herbert, Shepley
Audrey C B Hibbert
Barry Hill
Geoffrey Hill
Rose Miriam Hill
Theodore R Hill
John Allen Hinchliffe
Keith & Eileen Hinchliffe
Randall Hinchliffe
Mrs V Hinkley
Mrs Margaret S Hird
Arthur Hirst
David A Hirst
Mr & Mrs Jeff Hirst
Mr John Hirst
Mr & Mrs M W Hirst
Mr Richard S Hirst
David Hobson
Geoffrey Hodgson
Ted Holloway

Mr David John Holmes
Joyce & David Holroyd
David M Holt
Cynthia K Hooper
Rita Hopping
R Hough
Eric Howard
Billy Howe
Matthew P Hunt
Margaret Ingham
Susan R Ingham
Mr & Mrs R Inglesfield and Family
Clifford David Irving
Mr & Mrs E D Jackson
David Jenkins
Edward Jenkins
Brian Jenkinson
David P Jepson
E Jessop
Jacqeline Anne Jessop, née Wilson
Peter T Jessop
Mr A Stephen Jones
Ian R Jones
Jaqueline Jones
John A & Rita Kaye
Ken Kaye
Martin & Margaret Kaye
Philip & Anne Kaye
Richard & Ann Kaye
Eddie Keating
Mr B Kilner
Mr G Kilner
Kirklees Media Centre
Kitty Knowles
Betty & Nick Korol
Brian Lawton
Kathleen Laycock
Mrs Elaine C Lee
Michael R Leech
Joan Shirley Le Morellec
David Lewis
Barry Lockwood
Philip Lockwood
Alec Lodge
Richard George Lumb
James Macaskie
Mr Andrew John McDermott
Miss Philippa McGuinness
Ian & Elaine McKean
Ian McKenzie
Alex & Esther McNeil
M A McNulty
K Makin
Mr Rodney Marriott
Mrs Suzanne Martin
David Matthews
Christine M May
Sheila & Jack Maynard
Janet Mellor
Jim & Joyce Mellor
David Meredith
B & S Midwood
Charles Buchan Milne

M Milnes
David Mitchell
Ronnie & Janet Moorhouse
Shirley M Moorhouse
Stephen Moorhouse
Mr A Morton (York)
Paul M Mullany
Alan Murgatroyd
John, Glennis & Shaun Murphy
Peter T Nicholas
Danny Noble
Mr Trevor Noble
Shirley Norcliffe
Alfred North BEM
Paul Nugent
Richard Oates
Mr D M Oldfield
Mrs Jeanetta Oldfield
Mr C P Oldroyd
Mr E J O'Sullivan
Mrs Molly Owens
Mr David J Pack
Jennifer Palliser
Kenneth Palmer
Mike Parkin
Donald & Audrey Parkinson
Mr & Mrs G Peach
Frank Pearson
Miss N Pearson
Mr G L Pilling
Ian A M Pogson
Michael E Pointon
Brian Polley
Mr K Porter
Raymond P Prior
Jack Quarmby
Raymond Radford
George Ramsay
Florence Raper née Bower
David Rawnsley
Mrs Hilary Patricia Reeves
Harold Rhodes
Phillip Rhodes
Eric & Jean Richardson for Gemma & Fay
Judith & Martin Richardson
Mrs Ripley & David
Mrs Dorothy M Roberts
Josephine Roberts
John Robinson
Mr F Rockett
Rev S W Roebuck
Clifford Rothery
Mrs Maureen Roughton
Elizabeth S Sanderson (Hunt)
Thelma Saville
Mr Andrew George Schofield
Mrs Dorothy Schofield
J P Senior
Mr Ramon Senior
Sydney Senior
Jacqui & Derek Sewell
John F Sharp
Fred Shaw

Lance E Shaw
Mike & Shirley Shaw
Edgar Shepherd
Victor Shepherd
Mrs Iris Shields
Neil Shuttleworth
Adrian & Joan Sisson
J J & M Sloan – to commemorate our Ruby
  Wedding
Mr & Mrs C Smith
Eric Smith
G R Smith
Dr K E & Mrs W M Smith
Philip Charles Smith
Philip J Smith
Richard Stephen Smith
S V Smith
John & Sylvia Smithson
Audrey Snowdon
Major (Ret) R Speight
Joan Spencer
Mrs Barbara Spooner
Mr M A Stannard
N Stansfield
Violet Holdsworth Bentley Stead
Ghislaine & David Stephenson
Mrs Beryl Stockhill
A H Stocks
Len Storey
Steven Swallow
Connie Sykes
David Keith Sykes
Donald Sykes
Edward Carl & Daphne Sykes
Jonathan Mark & Sally Ann Sykes
Joyce Sykes
Kenneth Sykes
Stephen John Sykes
Stuart & Barbara Sykes
Tony Sykes
Mr Brian Tann
Mr B Tatchell & Mrs N Tatchell
Brian Taylor
Mrs Gwen Taylor
Mr James Taylor
Mr Joe Taylor
Kenneth Taylor
Kenneth & Betty Taylor
M E Taylor
Peter R Taylor
S Thomsen-Foor
Edward Thornton
Lynda Thwaites

Mr M J Tippen
Mr & Mrs H Tolson
S Tracey
Tricia
David Tucker
The Verlander Family
Paul & Hilary Wade
Mr & Mrs Brian D Wadsworth
Mr Gilbert N Wadsworth
Betty H Walker
Christine & Ian Walker
David Ian Hardy Walker
David Rodney Haws Walker
Joan Walker
John Alan Walker
David & Daphne Wallace
David John Ward
M Ward
Barry Watkinson
Cliff & Margaret Welsh
Wendy
J S Whitaker
Susan White
Marie Whitebread, née Rushworth
Frank Whitehead
H D Whitehead
Kathleen Whitehead
Mr Frank Whiteley
James Whiteley
Susan & John Whitfield
Mr Gordon Whittles
Mrs Annie Whitwam
Mr Alan Whitworth
Mr David Whitworth
Mr Peter G Whitworth
Robin & Janet Widdup (Australia)
Mr James C Wild
David J Wilkinson
Pam & Roger Wilkinson
Roy Wilkinson
Stephen Williams
Douglas Wilson
Maureen Wilson
Harriet Alexandra Wood
William Wood
Derek & Margaret Wright
Douglas G & Gillian R Wright
D F Wrigley
Derek Wyke
Celia Wylde
Austin Wylie
Zeneca Ltd